Manic Depression

By Lamia Islam

Table of Contents

Chapter 1

Stuck in a Moment

"I was unconscious, half asleep.
The water is warm 'til you discover how deep.
I was jumping, for me it was a fall.
It's a long way down to nothing at all."
— U2

I was lying in bed, unable to move, a cold numbness filling my body. I was terrified to wake up and gripped by overwhelming sadness.

When I finally found the courage to open my eyes, I was totally disoriented, unsure of who I was or where I had been the past few days. Or even how many days had passed. I had never felt so scared. I had been lost in a dark room for what seemed like an eternity.

Four white walls surrounded me and, except for the ticking of a clock, everything else was very still. The newspaper on my bedside was dated September 10th, 1998. *That has to be a printing mistake,* I thought. The last I remembered, it was September 4th and I knew that six days could not have simply evaporated. No, it's September 4th, I told myself. It must be.

I looked around, anxiety swelling up inside me, my heart racing and a sense that I couldn't breathe taking over. I realized that I was in my parents' room. The thick, green velvet curtains were drawn, but I could tell it was dawn, a sliver of light seeping through the large windows. The air felt heavy with gloom and all I could hear was the tick tock of that clock, which hung beside the bed's headrest like a giant wristwatch.

A white fan whirred gently from the high ceiling as I lay in the bed, which was made of Burma teak wood and had a headboard in the shape of a half moon. Matching night tables sat on either side. To the left was a wall with four, square windows and a wooden door that led to a terrace. Across the large room, was my father's desk with a neatly arranged row of books – mostly self-help books, but a few on religion and psychology. A beige rug was strewn on the white marble floor in front of the bed. Although my surroundings were familiar, I was lost. Totally lost.

Now, wide-awake from my sleep, I felt a deep emptiness. I vaguely recalled what had happened before I fell into a coma-like sleep, an intense, heavy sensation.

The last thing I remembered was arriving home my friend's house in an uncontrollable state of elation. It was the end of summer and my best friend Radeeya was leaving for the United States, set to get her master's degree at Texas A & M. For the last month, I had barely slept spending most of my time out with her and other friends playing poker, hanging out, drinking wine and smoking pot. Although my parents probably suspected what I was doing, they didn't say anything about my lifestyle. Even if they had, the rebel side of me didn't really care what they thought.

Feelings of happiness filled every part of my body. I was on top of the world, flying high to unreachable heights. Though I can't recall the specific words coming out of my mouth, I know I was saying things that made no sense, talking rubbish to anyone who would listen - all while feeling as if I was in total control. I had a level of confidence so ridiculous that even I was surprised. I felt as if I were a prophet sent to earth on a mission. I talked too much, laughed too loudly at every little thing and rambled on unnecessarily and uncontrollably. I blurted out my strange dreams to those around me – whether they wanted to hear them or not, feeling no sense of inhibition or discretion. I was needlessly happy and exhausting to my friends and family. My parents were confused by my behavior. But nothing could hold me back. Or so I thought.

I got ready to go out and called good-bye to my parents.

"You have to stay home," my mother said, as she stood by the stairs.

"You're not going out," my father added.

I thought they were joking, but they persisted, denying me access to the door. I was stunned. At this point in my life, I was a very independent 24-year-old. Although I lived in my parents' home, I was used to coming and going as I pleased. When my parents stood at the door forbidding me to leave, I knew something was wrong. I was confused. And the more they persisted, the more aggressive and furious I became, fighting my parents efforts to hold me back from my plans. But they must have sensed something about the trouble to come, like the wind that picks up a bit before an impending storm. They knew my uncontrollable state wasn't normal or natural. My parents did not have a clue as to what had turned a usually quiet and introverted girl into a nonstop talking machine.

Furious, I stormed off into my parents' bedroom and slammed the door so hard that the windows shook. Then I locked it behind me. (I was in my parents' room because mine was in a part of the house that was being renovated.) No matter how many times my parents or younger brother tried to talk to me or what they said, I wouldn't let them in the room. Finally, they stopped trying. Hours later, there was a knock on the door, a gentle knock that somehow I knew wasn't my family. I opened the door and saw a man standing there. He was casually dressed in slacks and a polo shirt with sandals.

Worried, puzzled and unable to understand my strange behavior, my parents had called a psychiatrist, named Dr. Mirza, to our home to conduct a medical exam and talk to me. I thought he looked familiar but couldn't place how I knew him. He gave me a hug and gently led me to the small, white sofa by the window. I didn't know his name or that he was a doctor, but I felt comfortable with him. He spoke quietly and then told me to close my eyes. Moments later I felt drowsy and as if I were floating in the air.

At the time I didn't realize that he had given me a sedative, all I knew was that my nerves had calmed. Then, I fell into a deep slumber. Any recollections about those days are disjointed. The time that passed was a blurry mess, as I went in and out of a heavy sleep never fully waking. Sometimes I felt it was daytime; others night, but I never knew the hour, the day, the moment. The only constant was the sound of that clock above the bed. I heard it's ticking, even when I was lost in days that were evaporating around me.

I went in and out of sleep, sometimes having strange dreams that shook me awake but that I couldn't remember. Sometimes my body felt heavy and hard to move. It was just me alone in blackness. From time to time, the silence was suddenly torn apart by the sounds of construction from the renovations in other parts of the house. I felt like I could relate to every single sound, like it was part of me. When the construction lorries arrived, I knew it was morning, but besides that I had no sense of time. Occasionally the sounds grew closer as my mother, father or the doctor opened the door and entered the room. I was barely aware of them, just felt a presence, a different energy around me and sensed the sliver of light briefly stretching into the room behind them when they opened the door.

I have vague memories of calling my best friend and leaving a message on her answering machine, talking on and on in incoherent ramblings until the machine cut me off. But it was as if I was in a fog. I can't tell you what came first and what came last. Amidst this fog, someone gave me medication, tiny pills in a little, paper cup. I hid the pills under my tongue for all those days. I don't know why I didn't want to swallow them, but I didn't. Unfortunately, I got a serious tongue infection from keeping all that medication hidden under my tongue.

At one point I remember answering the phone, certain that I was hearing the voices of two of my best friends, but there was actually someone else on the line. I am not sure who it was, but I heard my friends' voices – voices that weren't there. I was convinced of it.

I had never experienced anything like the overwhelming sadness that shrouded me when I woke those six days later. It enveloped me completely, holding me down with its gravity, wrapping me in its thick and gloomy fold. I didn't know where it was coming from, but it stayed with me for the weeks that followed. Now and again, I felt tiny, momentary surges of happiness, a sense of joy that gave me a thrill from within and then again, unexpectedly and suddenly, my heart would grow heavy.

Unable to believe that I had spent almost a week in a deep slumber, I called my friend Lamiza.

"What day is it?" I asked.

"The 10th of September," she replied.

I shook my head in disbelief, unwilling to surrender to the fact that I had lost six whole days of my life. I called two other friends, asking the same question and getting the same reply. A sensation of complete anxiety made my chest tighten. It was hard to breathe. *Why was I in that room alone? What had happened between the 4th and the 10th of September?* I wondered. The mystery of the missing days seemed unsolvable. *Was this some sort of a prank?* At most, I thought it had been two days.

No matter how hard tried, I could not explain what had happened to me; worst still, I could not remember who I was. The previous 24 years of my life seemed to have completely disappeared and were now a remote recollection. Very remote, as if I was thinking about someone else's life. The slate seemed empty. It felt like a new beginning, a new life. *Was I just being born?* Even worse, the girl I was before – confident, friendly, fearless and happy -was also totally gone, another distant memory. She was an acquaintance from my past. I felt tired and unloved. Nothing seemed meaningful.

Later I learned that the doctor had to sedate me because I was going through a manic episode. This was my first introduction to the illness that would become a part of my life, threatening to steal my soul and leave me lifeless and heavy-hearted, a veil of sadness following my every move.

Today, I think of my life in two distinct parts – before my illness and after. Before, I was a happy, go-lucky person. Normal. Not someone who could lose her mind. After? I didn't know who I was. What had happened? Why did I lose it? It seemed like I was no longer the girl I used to be.

Chapter 2
A Carefree Childhood

"Those were such happy times
And not so long ago
How I wondered where they'd gone."
–The Carpenters

My last clear image from before my illness was at a religious get-together to mark the anniversary of my uncle's death. I remember it completely. At the time, there was serious flooding in Dhaka and you couldn't drive your car anywhere. Because of the floods, the get-together took place at a compound of mansions where I had spent the first ten, joyful years of my life, a place my father owned that was about half an hour from where my mother, father and I lived at the time. On that day, I was absolutely fine, my normal, polite self. I could never have imagined the turn my life would take, the scariest journey of my life.

Before my illness, I could socialize with anyone. I always had very good friends, partly because I was a great listener – better at listening to others share their problems than revealing my own. I kept most of my own feelings to myself, but I still made strong connections with others. I was really fun and one of those people who others always wanted to be around.

The first ten years of my life were spent in a carefree way in that compound of five large homes where my father, his sisters and his brothers had grown up. Not only did I live with my parents, but amidst fourteen cousins, four aunts, four uncles and my paternal grandmother in the capital city of Bangladesh.

The compound consisted of five enormous houses. In fact, they were the biggest houses for miles around, more than six times the size of any other. Each one had what seemed like endless rooms on their three floors as well as two large kitchens, one upstairs and one downstairs. The compound also had one garage so huge that it could house more than 15 cars. Outside, there were over four acres of sprawling grounds. The five houses formed a circle with a vast courtyard in the center. In one area there was a fountain; in another, there was an amazing playground with slides and swings, a merry-go round. There was even a badminton court. To say it was a child's dream is an understatement.

Because there were so many of us children, we were a community of our own. At times neighbors would come over to play, but there really was no need to mingle with anyone outside our extended family. I didn't make any friends at school from about first grade until sixth because who needed friends when I had 14 cousins to spend time with? In the morning, all of us would get driven to our various schools – the boys to one school and the girls to another - in a huge, orange van. One of my cousins was in my class for three or four years so we'd play at recess and have snack together. At home, we were inseparable.

Every evening, after doing our homework, my cousins and I would meet outside to play soccer and badminton. At the time, I was quite a tomboy so I loved kicking a soccer ball around with my male cousins and playing other sports with them. (In our culture, boys and girls don't mingle once they get to be teenagers, but we were so young back then that there were no restrictions.) Since I was quite athletic and skilled at most sports, the boys always wanted me on their teams. Of course, I also played with the girls, things like cricket and board games. I loved being around so many people. I was never lonely and because we didn't need to be supervised within the safety of our family compound, we all had a sense of freedom. Life was carefree and seemingly perfect.

Our families employed a large staff to care for the houses, something that's very common because it's not as expensive to have help as it is in other countries. We had different people to cook, clean, drive, and take care of us, many of whom worked for my family for a very long time. One cook had been with my family since my father was in college. Although technically these people were our employees, they felt more like extended family. They were special. There was also a system that my mother and aunts had set up. Every two months, my mother would look after the big household issues, like figuring out what groceries we needed, what the cook should make for meals and directing the other people who cared for the houses. Then the next two months, one of my aunts would do that and so on. Of course, there were fights and arguments, but my mother and aunts were pretty proficient- especially when I look back and realize how young they were at the time.

Although we spent countless hours with my cousins, we also had our privacy. Sometimes, instead of eating meals with the entire extended family, the three of us would eat alone in our house. Or my father, mother and I would have dinner at my maternal grandmother's house and once a week we ate out at a restaurant.

I couldn't ask for a better way to live as a child and would have stayed there forever if we could. Unfortunately, we didn't. When I was ten-years-old, my father and his brothers decided that each of their families should move to houses that weren't so closely connected. None of the seemed particularly sad to part with their siblings, but I was devastated. The thought of living with just my mother and father seemed excruciatingly lonely. When we moved out of the compound, my grandmother would rotate houses, staying one month in our house and one month with each of my uncles. Eventually, she decided just to live with us.

Another care-free aspect of my childhood was money, a subject I never, *ever* thought about. From a very young age, I was aware that we were one of the richest families in Bangladesh and that everybody knew our family. Compared to other people, like my father's sisters and our next-door neighbors, we were very well off. We used to vacation twice a year, traveling everywhere from London to Thailand. Some of my cousins were jealous, but the money and our lifestyle didn't alter my view of other people. I never cared – and still don't - how much or how little anyone had. I went to a very good, all-girls school with people from really humble backgrounds. I could get along easily with all types of people and didn't have problems mixing with anyone whose race, social class or anything else was different from mine. Part of this was my parents' example, since they often invited people of various backgrounds to our house. In fact, the differences intrigued me.

In college, my friends used to have jobs – teaching or tutoring to make money, but I never needed to. When we would hang out and go for lunch or dinner, I'd pay the bill. I didn't do this because I felt sorry for them. I did it because I was happy to spend time with them. If they felt strange, they never let on. (Today, some of these friends insist on treating me whenever we go out because they feel that I treated them enough when we were younger.)

Chapter 3
Teenage Years

"When you're talkin' to yourself
And nobody's home
You can fool yourself
You came in this world alone."
- Guns 'n Roses

My mother was only 20 when she had me so when I look back at all that she handled, I think that she parented quite well for someone so young. But as a child, I saw my mother as imposing and dominating with a very short temper. I was an average student in school (more on that later) and my mother did not have high expectations for me. However, education was important to my parents so my mother used to teach me – in addition to school- when I was in second and third grade. Often, she would loose her temper during my lessons.

Although I'd always had a good relationship with my parents, things started getting complicated when I was a teenager. Since I was not good in studies, my mother put a lot pressure on me. I'm somewhat rebellious so, not surprisingly, the more pressure she put on me, the more I resisted. My parents are also very religious and because I was an obedient child, I used to believe whatever they told me to believe. I thought it was a sin to ask any questions about religion. But once I hit my teenage years, my mother pressured me to become more religious (which is probably why I'm not religious today). Silently, I began resenting her.

Over time, I started having a mind of my own and had questions that I knew I wasn't supposed to ask. No, I didn't have the courage to say anything to my mother for fear of getting scolded, but I used to rebel in my own way. For example, when she would teach me what *she* believed, I used to think about only what *I* truly believed. (Even today, as an adult I wouldn't tell my parents what I really think about religion. There is no point. It won't change their beliefs and would just hurt their feelings.) I created a secret world, which was only mine. I acted as if I were a dumb person who doesn't understand anything.

When we lived in the big complex of houses, my mother was very popular among my cousins, aunts, and grandmother. But she was so busy pleasing everyone that often she ignored me. One time stands out in my mind – a seemingly small moment that caused pain so deep. My father had bought me a brand-new board game. When my cousins got upset that they didn't have the same game, my mother pulled it from my hands and gave it to them. I was furious. But she didn't care.

I had to admit that my father was always my favorite and I wanted to be like him when I grew up. Even though he was a very busy businessman who travelled frequently, he spent a lot of time with us and was very patient and understanding. Before he would leave for a business trip, he would take my mother and me out for dinner. What fascinated me about him was that he had two sides to his personality. With his side of the family, he was very reserved and serious – so reserved that my cousins were a bit scared of him. With my mother's side of the family, however, he was jolly and funny. This was the part of his personality that I enjoyed the best. My father also never interfered in my life. He was -and still is- a genuine and honest person who has never, ever criticized me or imposed his thoughts or opinions on me. He never talks just for the sake of saying something. Instead, he has his own gentle way of expressing himself. Once, in the days before I got sick when I was in my twenties, I was going out a lot. I think my father suspected that I was doing things like drinking alcohol and smoking pot, but he didn't reprimand me or confront me harshly, two things that would have pushed me away. Instead, he gently said, "Take care of yourself, Nadera. There are a lot of bad things out there and you should stay away from them."

As a teenager, I was an easygoing person. Most people saw me as an "average" student, but my friendly nature and my athleticism made me quite popular amongst my peers. Though I mingled with most people around me, there was a part of myself that I could not share or explain to anyone.

From a very young age, I often had dreams about people who were close to me, an instinct about things that were going to happen. Many times these dreams came true and this haunted me. Once when I was about eight or nine, I had a dream that my great aunt on my father's side died. When my mother spoke to her later that day, we found out she was actually very ill. Another time, my father was travelling in the Middle East and I had a bad dream about him. Later that morning, we learned that he had been in a car accident. When I was 15 or 16-years-old, I had a dream about one of my cousins who I was very close to. At that time, she had gotten married and moved to the United States with her husband. I always felt that she was in pain and not happy and one night I had a dream that she ran away. About a month later, I found out that she had actually left her husband. I couldn't understand why I had these visions or how to explain them. The fact that many had some truth to them petrified me. Because it was so strange and scary, I suppressed them.

Looking back I think this denial contributed to me being manic years later because sometimes when you bury strong emotions so deeply, they come out in a strange way.

I don't think I had any dreams that predicted my illness although for some reason I *did* go to a psychiatrist without telling anybody. A friend was going through some emotional turmoil in her life and was seeing a psychologist. For some reason, I decided that I should go, too. And even before that, I started seeing my school college counselor. If you ask me why I went to her, I can't tell you. Nothing specific was bothering me or happening in my life. But clearly, something was bubbling beneath the surface.

Chapter 4
Comfortably Numb

"You are only coming through in waves
Your lips move
But I can't hear what you're saying...
I have become comfortably numb."
– Pink Floyd

Clearly, it all erupted from beneath the surface that September day when I woke from that hazy six days of sleep. In the time that followed, I found no interest in the things around me.

Worried and wanting the best medical care for me, my parents decided to take me to New York. They owned an apartment building in Long Island, New York so spending time and traveling there was relatively easy. They knew I could get better medical treatment there than in Dhaka and perhaps they thought the change in environment would help. Not thinking there was anything wrong with me, I assumed we were going to the States on vacation.

Although being in a manic state is not a good feeling for those around you, it's actually fun. That may sound strange and of course it is part of serious mental disorder, but in the moment you feel like you are on top of the world. There is no inhibition and you feel free, free, free. That's how I felt on the 22-hour plane ride from Dhaka to New York. I somehow convinced myself that everyone was looking at me in a good way, thinking I was famous and that they wanted to know me. I talked endlessly to anyone who paid attention to me, dominating every conversation. I felt each person's glance on me and it seemed that without me the world would stop revolving. I was above everyone. Of course, I was the only one who enjoyed that flight. For my parents, my behavior was stressful and very embarrassing.

But I didn't notice. I was so manic that I felt this deep connection to everything around me. I listened to music like John Lennon and Pink Floyd and felt so connected to each song, playing them over and over. Those feelings were so intense that even today I'm scared to listen to that music. I looked out the window watching the sunlight stream through the wispy clouds and felt connected to every single yellow ray. It seemed like the entire world was under my feet.

Once in New York, we went to the apartment my parents had in Long Island. I really wanted to go to graduate school and, in my manic state, was totally convinced that I could get into Columbia University on the spot, in an instant. I had graduated college in Dhaka. Besides that I didn't have any preparation. I hadn't taken my GREs, hadn't filled out an application or anything, but as manic as I was, I insisted it could happen. I was adamant about going to look at it. My parents wouldn't let me out of the house alone so my father and two of his friends took me to the Columbia University campus. Again, just like on the plane, I felt like everyone was watching and noticing me in a good way, like I was somebody special. I thought for sure I would get into the school.

A day or so later my parents told me that we had a doctor's appointment. I remember little about the ride to the city, except that my father's friend drove us from Long Island into Manhattan, about 20 minutes away. When we stopped, we were at Cornell Hospital, a world-renowned hospital in an upscale Manhattan neighborhood.

Although it's so hard to remember that time, there are a few little things that stand out. When we walked into the hospital, we were introduced to a nurse who began asking me a lot of questions. I was trying to explain the emotions inside of me, but felt like I wasn't making any sense. For some reason, I thought they were going to hypnotize me to make me better and I was actually excited. I'm not sure why I believed this because no one told me that, but there were a lot of things inside me that I wanted to express and I could not. *If they hypnotize me*, I thought, *these things will come out*. I also thought we were just going for an appointment, then going back home.

"Aren't you going to hypnotize me?" I finally asked the nurse.

She glanced over at my parents with a puzzled expression. Then she turned back to me. Without saying a word and with a look of pity on her face, she shook her head. I looked at my mother, but she had no idea what I was talking about. My stomach sank. In that moment, I knew something was terribly wrong.

"You're going to stay in the hospital," the nurse told me.

"What?" *I'm not ill. So why am I staying in a hospital?* I couldn't wrap my brain around what she was saying. I started crying. *There's nothing wrong with me,* I thought.

"I don't want to stay," I screamed, turning to my mother, certain she would say that she was taking me home. But she just gave me a forced smile.

"You have to," she said. "Just for a little while." Then she left. Knowing my mother, I now realize how scary and difficult that moment must have been for her – to leave her only daughter in a hospital in another country. Today, I see that it also may have been a relief. Still, at that time and in that moment, I wasn't thinking about what *she* was feeling. Instead, I was furious with her for putting me in the hospital and for making me feel trapped. I had no idea what was going on. I later learned that my parents didn't know I was going to be admitted either. They had simply taken me in to see a doctor and once I started talking, it was clear to the nurse that something was seriously wrong with me.

Even worse, I had never stayed in the hospital before in my life. I was terrified by this new experience – an experience I didn't want to have. What happened next is a blur, but I do have a memory of being in a pale, worn, hospital gown.

"Get on the scale please," a different nurse said looking at her clipboard. I stepped on and, though I was still wearing socks, I could feel the scale's cold metal beneath my feet. A chill ran through me. The nurse moved the weights on the scale back and forth in rough, jerking movements until finally it was balanced.

"Ninety four pounds," she announced. *Ninety-four pounds?* I thought. *I'm dying.* I hadn't weighed ninety-four pounds since grade 7. Normal for me was about 105. My stomach twisted into knots and a heaviness filled my chest.

The next thing I remember I was in a hospital room alone, waking up from a deep sleep. I was wearing faded jeans and a checked, button-down shirt that I didn't recognize. I didn't know what time or day it was. But even worse was the room. Everything in it was foreign to me and everything was cold. The walls were painted beige, cracked and chipped in some areas. The bed was metal, with sides that could move up and down and the mattress was so thin I could practically feel the metal beneath me. I was lying on top of a worn gray sheet covered by a light, woven blanket. The air was sterile and stale. The room had its own bathroom that had the lingering scent of disinfectant in the air. Nothing was warm. It was unwelcoming. It was the last place I wanted to be. *I am not a drug addict or an alcoholic, so what am I doing here?* I wondered. *Am I being treated for madness?* The thought made me feel suddenly weak and totally alone.

For me, it was like I was in a jail. I couldn't do things that I wanted to do. I had to listen to whatever the doctors and nurses told me. Also, there was no lock on the door, which was always slightly ajar so I felt like a prisoner with no privacy. I felt so out of control of my own life. In the blink of an eye, I had become a child again. I had lost 24 years of my life. *What the hell happened?* I wondered. The emotions inside of me were so unfamiliar and as a result so scary and confusing.

The other patients were a mix of different ages and ethnic backgrounds. No one stands out to me because I interacted with them as little as possible. In fact, I went out of my way to avoid them. There were plenty of girls around my age, but I wanted nothing to do with them. Once I entered the hospital, something changed in me. Gone was the chatty, talkative girl from the plane. Gone was the manic side. Suddenly, I became really quite and withdrawn. Just saying "hello" to anyone set my heart racing. This was amazing to me since my whole life I had been outgoing and very comfortable with others. But my confidence was so low that I didn't want to talk to anyone – especially a group of total strangers. Whatever I said would be stupid, so why say anything at all? Wouldn't they just laugh at me? Every interaction was a struggle.

My days there consisted of seeing a psychiatrist, Dr. Simon who I didn't like at all. She was extremely thin with dark, curly hair and very sharp features. There was something about her appearance that was cold. She was very formal and clinical. I had been in the hospital about a week, seeing her every day, sometimes twice a day for private therapy sessions and for her to monitor my medication. I felt very close to her so after one particular session, I reached out to hug her when the session was over.

"No hugging allowed in the hospital," she said stiffly. *No hugging? I thought. How can I connect with these people when this place is so cold?* I felt unwelcomed and even more alone. I was supposed to attend group therapy, but after just one session, I didn't go back. I couldn't explain what I was feeling to myself. How could I explain it to a room full of strangers? I had never been worried about what other people thought of me, but now I felt like an idiot around them.

Once a day, I would call my best friend, Radeeya, who was in graduate school at Texas A & M. Back then they didn't have cell phones, so I'd call her collect. She was a struggling student, but she accepted my call every time. Those calls were the highlight of my day, but the hospital had restrictions on when you could use the phone. It was like jail.

One thing I *did* care about was gaining weight. I was petrified of how thin I'd become and I didn't recognize myself in the mirror. I thought gaining weight would make me healthy and being healthy would mean I could leave that horrible place. But the hospital food was so bland that I couldn't eat it. Instead, my parents brought me lunch and dinner – sometimes Bangladeshi food, sometimes Chinese - during their daily visits. My mom would also take my clothes, wash them and bring them back to me. She and my father put on a good face for me and acted strong and casual during our visits, although they probably went home feeling miserable. They would meet with some of my doctors privately and then come and sit with me. They never asked me what was going on or how I felt. They tried to act normal like they were just visiting me at a hotel or something, but I am sure it brought them deep pain and sadness.

Twice a day, I'd line up with the rest of the patients at this counter in the corner of the communal area to get my medicine. A nurse would watch me take it out of the tiny, paper cup, put it in my mouth and swallow it, monitoring my every move. It was exactly like a scene from the movie *One Flew Over the Cuckoo's Nest* and I felt very ashamed.

There was no TV in my bedroom, but there was one in the common area where the other patients would watch shows and they hospital would show movies. There was also a ping-pong table, checkers and other board games, but I was not interested in doing anything. Instead, I sat on the thin, tiny bed in my room for hours on end, all alone. I didn't read or listen to music. Instead, I sat there with my thoughts and this horrible weight that was buried in the center of my stomach. It truly seemed like one minute I was living my happy-go lucky life as a confident, in control girl and the next I woke up in the hospital.

To say I was depressed is an understatement. The sense of loneliness ran deep. It was like I was seeing my life before this, the "old" me, like a movie, but couldn't imagine being that girl. I was so eager to get out of that hospital, constantly asking my psychiatrist, "When am I going home?"

"You have to stay a little longer," she would answer. When I'd ask the nurse, she'd say, "The doctor will tell you."

"I want to go home," I told my parents when they came to visit.

"Soon," they would say. But "soon" felt like it would never come.

When that day finally arrived, a weight started to lift off my shoulders. I thought once I passed through the hospital's glass sliding doors, that weight would evaporate completely and I would feel like myself again. When I didn't, when the same feeling of gloom surrounded me, my mood plummeted. A horrible sensation filled my chest, one that I can't even explain. It was heavy and foreign like I was suffocating.

Chapter 5

Empty & Turned to Stone

"Ice is forming on the tips of my wings
Unheeded warnings, I thought, I thought of everything
No navigator to find my way home
Unladened, empty and turned to stone."
- Pink Floyd

When I got to my parent's Long Island apartment, it was clear that nothing had changed inside of me. This was a horrible realization that just made me more depressed.

What made it worse was that my parents were treating me like a child, I had to take a lot of medication and my parents were in charge of it. My father would sit there to watch me take it. (I guess they didn't trust me because I'd hidden medicine under my tongue when I first got sick back in Bangladesh.) And it was my parents who took me to my doctor's appointments. They barely let me out of their sight. On top of this, my mother was constantly monitoring what I ate since I had lost so much weight. Of course, their intentions were good, they only wanted me to get better. But this, combined with the fact that we were living in a small three-bedroom apartment was very suffocating. I was used to living with them in a huge house where I had lots of room and privacy. In New York, there was too much interaction because it was so small and they were afraid to leave me alone for a second.

Before that horrible September day I was an independent person, a mentally healthy adult. I was someone who was very in control of my life and my emotions. I was strong. I was logical. *I* was the one people turned to because I helped solve their problems. Suddenly, *I* had the problems. It was like I was two-years-old again.

Where had my once independent 24-year-old self gone?

They didn't say anything, but I could tell how concerned my parents were about me by the way they looked at me, by the glances that passed between them and in how eager they were to please. After all, my parents thought I was going to die so they were just happy that I was conscious. They would have done anything for me. For example, before I got ill I used to smoke cigarettes, which my parents hated. Now, I was adamant that I wanted smoke.

"You can't smoke," my mother said one time. But her tone was weak, more like a question than a statement.

"Yes, I can," I told her. She didn't protest. Instead, my mother went to the store and bought me a pack of cigarettes. It was my parents' way of trying their best to give me comfort.

Nighttime was the happiest for me. It felt like it belonged to me and me alone. At night, life was not as burdensome as it was during the day. I didn't have to face anyone, make conversation or pretend that I was the confident girl I had once been. I liked the quiet and stillness of the world and how the darkness outside of me seemed to match the darkness inside of me. Strangely, I felt more in harmony with myself during those quiet moments. Nearly everyone was asleep and there were no rude intruders, no one to bother me, no one to interact with and feel like a total idiot in front of. I didn't have to face the world. I was awake most of the night, but during the day, I wanted only to sleep. I would lie in bed, tossing and turning in a haze of various stages of sleep, blankets twisted around me, and the faint sounds of the world in the distance.

In the weeks and days after the hospital, the hyper, manic Nadera was gone. Now I was very quiet and disturbed. I was like a zombie. Part of this was because I was taking so much medication. Trying to snap me out of it, my mother would take me to places with a lot of people like Times Square, the Metropolitan Museum and Broadway shows. But these situations were unbearable for me. I was under so much medication that I couldn't focus and my reaction time was slow. Being around people made me nervous because I did not know what to say or how to act. I was so ashamed of myself and didn't want anyone to know that I'd been in the hospital or that I was ill.

In our culture being hospitalized for psychiatric reasons was not common so I was convinced that I was the only person on earth who had this illness. I wish someone had told me at the time how many people struggled with this illness, how many smart and accomplished people of all ages, races and classes. Honestly, at the time, I would have rather have had people think that I had a drug or alcohol problem than this mental illness.

Back then, I actually knew almost nothing about depression. Growing up, anyone with any mental issues was called "retarded." That was the only word I heard. (Today, that word has a totally different meaning.) Anything else I'd known about it came from one advertisement on Bangladesh television that I saw when I was in college. It was an ad about depression in which a lady who was clearly very upset sat in a rocking chair, slowly moving back and forth with a blank look in her eyes. At the end, a voice-over talked about where you should go if you're experiencing these very sad emotions. This ad created so much uproar and commotion in our community because many people claimed that after seeing it they actually felt depressed. As a result, the government banned this ad. When I saw it I was confused. *What are they talking about?* I thought. *And why would someone go to a doctor if they felt sad?* Around the same time, I remember a friend mentioning that people in the United States went to counseling. *Are these people so busy they don't have time to talk to friends or family?* I wondered. It seemed so strange to me. Now that I think about it, I hadn't even heard the words "mental health" before. But then I found myself fighting for mine.

The only thing I had to do in those days and weeks after the hospital was take medication daily, have my blood drawn weekly so they could manage my medication and see a psychiatrist twice a week. Her name was Dr. Churchin and she had been referred to me by the hospital. One of her jobs was to monitor the various medications that I was on and adjust them when needed. I was also supposed to meet with her twice a week for talk therapy. One of my parents would take me to my appointments in order to make sure that I went and we would sit together in silence in the car ride from our apartment to the city. They they would settle into the waiting room until I was finished. I hated these appointments because I didn't think I needed a psychiatrist and each visit reminded me that I was ill.

Dr. Churchin's office was in the same hospital I'd spent those horrible 24 days. The room had a single chair where she sat and a couch where I sat. There were a lot of books, a desk and a window with a view of the Queensboro Bridge. From the first appointment, I felt uncomfortable in Dr. Churchin's presence and the cold, formal aura that surrounded her and this didn't change even after months and months of our meetings. She seemed distant and rigid and I could not open up to her. The 45-minute sessions seemed to last too long and I felt like I had nothing to say. I just wanted to go back to Bangladesh and start my life all over again. I wanted it all to end. Thinking that I was suffering from a temporary illness brought with it some relief. I was under the illusion that the treatment received at the hospital and days spent as an outpatient would be effective and consoled myself that I would be fine soon.

Most days I would walk into Dr. Churchin's office and she would give me her usual nod hello. I remember one time in particular.

"How are you?" she asked in more of a routine way rather than as a question of concern.

"Fine," I said. "I'm fine."

"You're not fine. Why are you saying you're fine?" she said briskly. I dreaded those sessions and spent most of them staring at my watch, wishing its hands would move more quickly so I could leave. She asked me a lot of questions, which I hated because I had nothing to talk about. I didn't understand what I was feeling or what was wrong with me so how could I explain it or share it with someone else? Often I didn't stay for the full 45 minutes. After about twelve sessions, I asked her, "When am I going to stop my medication? How much longer?"

"You're not going to stop," she said.

"What do you mean?" I said, my voice shaking. After all, my illness was a temporary thing. Wasn't it?

"Nadera, you have to take this medication for the rest of your life," she said casually like it was no big deal. *The rest of my life? What was she saying?* I didn't believe her.

"You have bipolar disorder so your moods go up and down," she said, using her hands to mimic an undulating, wave-like motion. "The medication keeps your moods in the middle." The news was devastating. I felt totally shattered.

In that instant, my life had changed.

Dr. Churchin continued talking, but I didn't hear anything else that she said for the rest of the session because I was so shocked and so ashamed. *What is wrong with me? How can I face this world with this illness?* I wondered.

I had been so healthy my entire life, never hospitalized for anything and the only medication I ever took was a rare Tylenol here and there. Even the few times I was prescribed an antibiotic, I never even finished the course. Medication was not part of my world. To me, it was something you took if you were very old like my grandmother or if you had a serious illness like my uncle who had diabetes. But *me*, take medicine *forever*? I could not fathom needing to do so for the rest of my life. I could not accept that I was never going to be the same girl that I used to be.

I had thought the medication was a temporary thing, something I'd take for a few weeks or months. Then I'd be fine and go back to my normal life. I couldn't stop staring at the bridge out the window. Dr. Churchin was talking, but I interrupted her.

"Why did this happen to me?" I asked.

"Genetics," she said. "Bipolar disorder is a genetic thing."

"What?" I shook my head. "No one in my family has this. There must be another reason." Dr. Churchin just shrugged and raised her eyebrows. I left her office feeling furious and even more confused. *I'm not buying this genetic thing,* I thought.

However, weeks, months and even years after this pivotal moment in my life, I started connecting the dots. I looked back and *did* see this illness in my family; I'd just never had a name for it.

Growing up, my father was very moody, going in and out of dark periods at uneven intervals. Sometime he was really up. Other times, so down that there was nothing any of us could do to pull him out. I even remembered a story that I grew up hearing about him. It was this family joke about a time when my father lost a lot of money from a business deal. Apparently, he wouldn't talk to anyone for weeks. My uncles joked that he had a nervous breakdown. Although they laughed it off, I realized now that it was a form of depression, probably bipolar disorder.

I also remembered how, during a certain time of the year, my father's mother used to get sick. I don't know exactly what it was, but my grandmother stayed in her bed for long periods of time. My aunts, too, had this kind of problem that had no name. One of my cousins used to joke that we had a "pagol family." "Pagol" in Bangla means mad.

There was also one day when I was eighteen years old. We had a neighbor whom my mother was very, very close to. She was a really warm, happy, confident person. One day she came to our door and she was completely disoriented. She didn't know where she was and she didn't recognize anyone, not even my mother. I was so confused.

"What's wrong with her?" I asked my mother. "I saw her a few days ago and she was absolutely fine." That was the first shock in my life, to see someone who was normal become like that. It freaked me out. I asked another neighbor what happened and she said, "Sometimes that happens to her, but then a few days later she's herself again."

Unfortunately, that story and all my dot connecting didn't come back to me until I was actually writing this book. So at the time, in 1998, when I was sitting in that hospital and in that doctor's office and in my parent's home in Long Island, I honestly thought I was the only one in the world who had this mental illness. I felt utterly lost and alone and ashamed.

During that time, my mother pushed me to invite people over. Of course, her intentions were good: she wanted to help me and to see me laugh and smile again. She wanted to revive the old me, the girl who could socialize with anyone. But seeing people was an enormous struggle for me because I didn't have any confidence. *I am so stupid,* I thought. *So how can I talk to anyone?* The worst thing about this was that talking to people had never been an issue for me. My whole life, I could talk to anyone no matter their age, class, or status. I could engage in conversation with friends, acquaintances and total strangers. I don't mean to sound boastful, but I was someone people always loved to talk to. Friends and cousins confided in me. Now, just making small talk was stressful. I worried about what I would say to the people my mother was inviting to visit us.

Over time, many of my cousins, friends and my sister-in-law came from all different cities to stay with us for two to three day visits. Normally, that would have thrilled me, the "old" me that is, but it was horrible. I didn't know what to do with them or in front of them. I was convinced that I was making a fool of myself all the time. I had inhibitions and fears – new emotions that were so scary. I longed to be the carefree girl I was before, the one who took her ease with people, with life, and her confidence for granted.

At times someone would say, "Why are you so quiet?" If it was someone I had known before my illness, I felt foolish like I wasn't living up to their expectations of me.

One of our visitors was my best friend Radeeya. We had known each other since we were in the sixth grade and at the time she lived in Texas. About a week after I was discharged from the hospital, my mother was on the phone with her.

"Why don't you come to New York City for a long weekend?" I heard my mom ask her. "We'll pay for your ticket."

"Oh good!" my mother said moments later so I knew that Radeeya had said yes. My parents were thrilled that she was coming, hoping that seeing an old, close friend would snap me back into the daughter they used to know. But I was nervous. I couldn't pretend to be someone I was not and certainly this unfeeling zombie was not who Radeeya expected to see.

"I don't want her to come," I told my mother.

"Don't worry," she said. "When Radeeya comes, you'll be laughing all the time just like you used to."

I wasn't so sure. I put a huge amount of pressure on myself to be the same exact person I was before my illness, the friend she'd known for years. Looking back now I realize that of course that's not what Radeeya expected. She knew I was sick, very sick. She knew it was serious and that I wasn't going to just bounce back in a matter of days or even weeks. That's exactly *why* she was coming to visit. She expected nothing from me, yet I was so insecure I didn't see that.

Also, because it was Radeeya's first time in New York City, I wanted to show her so many things like the Empire State Building, the Statue of Liberty, the Metropolitan Museum of Art and Central Park. Before my illness giving her a tour of these famous landmarks would have been thrilling. But I did not have the energy or confidence to take her anywhere. It was still hard for me to be with other people and this was an added pressure.

When she arrived, I could tell that she shocked to see me because I had lost so much weight. Besides that, she didn't let on that she felt I was different. She was warm and supportive. Luckily another friend of ours who lived in New Jersey also came to visit. I'm not sure if my mother arranged this or not, but having this friend and her husband come with me to take Radeeya sight-seeing was a huge relief. Gone was the pressure to be the sole entertainer. I just went along and didn't plan anything. That part was better than I thought although I still felt uncomfortable.

During Radeeya's visit, we saw two popular, award-winning Broadway shows, *Rent* and *Phantom of the Opera*. As we watched these performances, sitting in these two different ornate, beautiful old theaters, I saw how much my friends were enjoying them. After the show, they talked nonstop about what we saw, about the shows' messages, the sets, the story, etc. They couldn't get enough.

But me? Well, I didn't understand anything. It was as if we had seen totally different shows. *I'm so stupid,* I thought. *And getting stupider everyday.* Having my best friend visit should have been a comfort, but in some ways I was getting more stressed. She was my closest friend and yet I couldn't talk to her about what I was feeling. It wasn't that she would judge me or make me feel bad. No. I knew that she would have understood and been compassionate, but how could I talk about something that I was struggling to understand myself? I also felt that I wasn't living up to my friend's expectations and that I was a very different person than before. When Radeeya left, I felt exhausted.

In the weeks after her visit, I was still like a zombie. Time felt like it was not moving. I had a gold Cartier watch with a maroon leather strap. It had a tiny second hand and for me, everything was still except that second hand. The only thing that kept me moving was my watch. I would stare at it thinking to myself, *This thing is moving. That's how much time is passing.* That watch was everything to me back then. I rarely turned on the television because I couldn't understand what they were talking about. I couldn't concentrate. I couldn't focus. Nothing made sense. I spent a lot of time alone doing nothing.

The only thing I *did* want to do –besides sleep - was eat because I was still haunted by the fact that I was 94 pounds. After I came back from the hospital, my goal was to gain weight so I was eating like crazy. This wasn't hard to do because my appetite was huge thanks to the antidepressant I was taking. I loved burgers and pizza and pretty much anything because I was hungry all the time. Sometimes if I couldn't sleep, I would sneak quietly down to the kitchen and eat in the middle of the night. Another reason why I ate was because it was one of the few sensations I could actually feel.

Before I got ill, I was a very compassionate person. If someone was in pain, I was in pain. If a friend was sad, I was sad, too. But after my illness I was totally numb. I literally forgot how to feel. During that time, my maternal grandmother died. I had loved her very much and was really close to her. We had spent a lot of time with her growing up and throughout my childhood we ate dinner at her house at least once a week. But I didn't cry at her funeral. I *wanted* to be sad, to feel *something*, but I didn't feel *anything*. Unfortunately, this feeling would last for a while which was horrible because it put a distance between me and other people, sending me further and further into my own world. The only sensations I felt were the taste of the food and the only thing that I could get some satisfaction from was eating. Just a month after getting out of the hospital, I was up to 125 pounds. My parents took the fact that I was eating and putting on weight as a sign that I was healthy. But this extra weight made me even more depressed.

My father had a business in New York and he wanted me to work for him. None of it was hard work, just simple things like filing and organizing. I think his intentions were to put my focus somewhere else besides my illness, but it didn't work. I would go to his office with him, but once I got there I felt clueless and helpless. I couldn't understand what was going on or what I was supposed to do. Even the smallest task made me feel like an idiot. My confidence plummeted even more – if that was even possible. My father never pressured me and clearly it was the pressure I put on myself that made the situation so bad, but either way, it didn't work out.

About two months after being hospitalized, my parents and I went to a relatives' house for dinner. These were relatives we were close to and who had known me my whole life. Just seven or eight months earlier, before my illness, I'd actually stayed with them for a few days. During that first visit, I told stories that made them laugh and was jolly and outgoing. What they didn't know was that this time they'd invited the "new" me to dinner. I was very quiet and didn't say anything except a mumbled hello. They had no idea about my illness so they were confused. All they saw was the drastic contrast between the girl who was always smiling and chatty, to a quiet, withdrawn one who couldn't crack the smallest smile.

"Nadera, why are you so quiet?" they asked.

"What's wrong?" Their concern was genuine and they didn't mean to make me uncomfortable, but they did. The more they asked, the more pressure I put on myself to be what they expected and the more anxious I got. I remember the look of my eyes back then. I had always been told I had expressive eyes, but now they were blank. I saw it when I looked in the mirror and I knew my relatives saw it, too. They weren't the only ones who couldn't relate to me. I couldn't relate to myself.

Chapter 6
Frozen Tree Trunk

"Ticking away the moments that make up a dull day
Fritter and waste the hours in an off-hand way
Kicking around on a piece of ground in your home town
Waiting for someone or something to show you the way."
- Pink Floyd, Time

The weeks went by and I remained enclosed within my shell. I was unable to do the things I normally did. I was very nervous around people besides my parents and could barely hold a conversation. Even small talk was excruciatingly painful. I thought everything I was saying was stupid. Nothing inspired me. I felt like a zombie.

The months that followed would be the most terrible five months of my life. I was an outpatient, doing regular counseling, but I hated every minute of it. I still could not connect to my psychiatrist. I had signed up for a six-week, two day a week real estate course to keep me busy and shift my focus, but I couldn't cope. I was so uncomfortable around so many people – there were about 50 in the class. You had to interact and answer questions, which felt impossible.

I could not understand what the professor was saying so I decided to skip classes and spend the morning hours in Central Park, giving my brain some rest and staring into space. I could do nothing and feel nothing. The peaceful surroundings in the park and the lush green trees seemed to soothe my soul. I felt safer and happier there, in company of the ducks and birds. I did not find the motivation or clarity of mind to continue with my studies. The course was a disaster and soon I dropped out.

My college convocation was coming up in December and I really wanted to go. I felt strongly that being back in Dhaka was the only way that things would be normal again. I was convinced that once I returned home, in a familiar place where the "old" me had lived, I would put this strange experience behind me and start my life over again. My friends, family and all that was familiar awaited me in Dhaka. To me, they were like a rewind button that would take me back to the "old" me.

Another month went by and though nothing had changed in my condition, I made arrangements to leave New York and return to Dhaka, despite my parents insistence that I stay put. But once they realized how serious I was, they arranged to come with me. I went there for three weeks, but contrary to my expectations, the emptiness within me grew deeper. I could not connect to those around me. People I got along with in the past seemed estranged and distant. I could not even open up with my best friends. I felt completely numb. I had nothing to say to anyone and was extremely anxious when anyone tried to converse with me. I could not understand what people were saying and did not know how to answer them. The pressure to be my "old" self and to perform like I used to was too much for me.

Instead, I would sit still for hours in one place without uttering a word. My friends started making fun of me and called me "brikkho Manobi" a Bangla word, which literally means "a frozen tree trunk." I probably earned this title due to the emptiness in my eyes and the fact that I would stare into space for hours on end. I was stiff in mind and body and couldn't function.

I wasn't the same person I was before. I couldn't relate to the things that my peers were doing in their lives – attending graduate school, working and getting married. A few times, friends said things like, "Nadera, remember when we did …" and the story they'd tell about me was shocking. Shocking, not because it was scandalous or dangerous, shocking because the girl they described was happy, confident and fun. Yes, I'd smile and nod at their stories. But inside, I'd think, *I said that*? or *I did those things*? This only made me feel worse.

The actual convocation ceremony was tiresome. I had been looking forward to this event, but my enthusiasm had completely disappeared, my confidence shattered when the day actually came. I wore my gown, held my degree and pretended to smile, but my soul was not in my body. I seemed to be in another world and nothing made me happy. I just wanted the ceremony to end as soon as possible.

The whole trip tortured me. Discovering that the "new" me was still there was devastating and made worse by the fact that she didn't mesh with the surroundings that the "old" me had apparently thrived in. I wanted to go back to New York so I didn't have to face the ghosts of my past. In fact, I never wanted to go back to Dhaka.

Chapter 7

Sudden Death

"Life is what happens
when you're making other plans."
– John Lennon

My convocation should have been a happy time, yet for me it was a disaster. I should have been celebrating my hard work in college. But looking back I see that it was actually my time in college that contributed to my illness. It didn't cause it, but it was the time where tiny, little fissures began to form in my psyche. When added together, I believe, they caused me to break down.

The first of these was the tremendous but secret guilt I carried with me when my cousin, who was one of my closest friends died tragically and unexpectedly. Nazia was just a year older than me and from as far back as I can remember she was in my life. In fact, my earliest memory is from the age of four and in it Nazia and I are sitting in the grass opposite each other with our little legs straddled. We're wearing matching shiny black shoes and white socks and we're rolling a brightly colored plastic ball back and forth between us, giggling each time the ball comes our way.

As children, Nazia and her family lived in one of the houses in the big compound that I mentioned earlier. It was her mother, father and three older brothers. Since neither of us had a sister and I had no siblings, we were like sisters to each other. We were together every chance that we got. Sometimes our other female cousins got jealous of our bond and irritated by all our private jokes and secrets. We tried not to leave anyone out, but the fact that the connection we had was deeper than what we shared with our other cousins was undeniable. All of us girls went to school together and Nazia and I always sat next to each other in the big van on the ride there in the morning. At night, the minute I was finished with my homework and tutors, I rushed to the courtyard in the center of all of our houses to find Nazia,.

I was also extremely close to Nazia's mother, my Aunt TK name. And actually, as a child, I loved her more than my mother. Of course, I kept this to myself for fear of offending my own mother, but it was true. There was just something about the way my aunt treated me that was different than any other adult. She didn't act like I was a bothersome child, but instead made me feel like she was truly listening and interested, not distracted or irritated. She looked me in the eye when she spoke rather than talking down to me – bother literally and figuratively. She always remembered every detail and kept any secret I shared.

When I was ten-years-old, we moved out of that big compound of houses. I was devastated. Who wouldn't? I was going from having more than a dozen constant playmates to living just with my small, immediate family. But even worse was that I felt like I was torn away from my *real* family: Nazia and my aunt. We still saw each other often at school and got together as families, but it wasn't the same in terms of how much time we could spend together. There wasn't the freedom or endless hours together. Now we had to make plans. Despite this, our sisterly bond stayed strong.

Although I began making friends at school- something I had felt no need to do when we lived in the family compound – Nazia was still the first person I told anything to, the keeper of all my secrets. As teenagers we turned to one another when our parents were driving us crazy and we wanted to rebel and we shared everything from our crushes to our hopes for the future. Even when we went to different colleges, we saw each other all the time and introduced one another to our new groups of friends. I told Nazia things that I had never told anyone.

Then when I was around 20 or 21, Nazia's father and my father (who were brothers) had a huge falling out over a business deal. Although I never learned the details of their argument, what was once a prosperous partnership had turned into a disaster. They had lost a large amount of money and each one blamed the other. I remember it was a Friday evening and we were supposed to have dinner with my Nazia and her family. I couldn't wait – especially because Nazia said she had some fun news to share. But all of a sudden while I was getting dressed to go, I heard my father talking loudly to my mother, almost shouting, which was something my soft-spoken father rarely did. I walked toward their bedroom, but the door was shut. A minute later my mother emerged.

"We'll eat dinner at home tonight," she said.

"What?" I said, stunned. We never cancelled plans with our relatives – especially Nazia's family. "Why not?"

"We'll talk about it later," my mother said. I rushed to call Nazia. She didn't understand what was going on either.

Later, I learned about the falling out and that something had happened that day that was the final straw for my father. I didn't think it would last. *They're family,* I thought. *You can't stop talking to family.* But we did.

Initially, my cousin and I tried to remain close. We swore we wouldn't let our fathers' business problems come between us. We still made plans when we had free time and on the weekends. But something had changed. I didn't feel comfortable when I went to Nazia's house anymore. My beloved Aunt slowly pulled away from me. She wasn't mean to me; she just wasn't herself. The warmth was gone. The special feeling evaporated. She never looked me in the eyes. It was a distancing that hurt so deeply, especially because at this time in my life, my parents didn't seem to understand me and my aunt always had.

Eventually, the fissure in our tight-knit family seeped into my relationship with Nazia, like a crack in a wall that starts at the ceiling and slowly spreads toward the floor. In a heated moment, she'd say something about my father that hurt; I'd retaliate with something about her parents. We barely knew what we were talking about, but one thing was sure: our relationship would never be the same. One afternoon, we got into an uncomfortable discussion about how things had changed.

"It's your father's fault," she blurted out. "All this is his fault." I didn't say a word, but after that I knew I'd lost my sister. It was like a death. I remember lying in my bed for days, feeling a gaping hole where my relationship with Nazia had once been. I'd never known life without her. What would it be like?

Six months went by. We barely saw Nazia's family at social events, but if we did, our family stayed on one side of the room and they stayed on the other. I couldn't even look at Nazia or I felt my heart would break. Then one day at college, I was talking with a new girl from a neighboring town. She casually said something about how nice I was.

"Why wouldn't I be?" I asked.

"I heard all these things about you, that you were spoiled and irresponsible," she said. As she went on and on, sharing all the things she'd heard about me, I realized the source of these horrible words was my aunt. (I knew this because there were details in her stories that only my aunt and Nazia would know.) The more this new girl told me, the wider that old wound opened. I was so hurt by the negative things they were saying about me. I couldn't believe it. I swore never to talk to anyone from that family again. I admit that after that I spoke badly about them, too. It wasn't the right thing to do, but I felt so betrayed.

About a month later, I got a call from my cousin. I couldn't believe it was her voice on my answering machine. Part of me wanted to dial her number right away; but another was so hurt, so angry and so betrayed that I deleted the message. A few weeks later, she left another message telling me that soon she was leaving for graduate school in Canada.

"I want to talk before I go," she said. Again, I deleted the message. I'd talk to her when I was ready and at this point, I wasn't.

Two weeks later, my mother woke me in the middle of the night.

"Nazia was in a car accident," she said, tears in her eyes. "She's dead." I thought I was in the middle of a horrible dream, but when I saw my father standing there, too, I knew it was real. I barely made it to the bathroom where I vomited and then passed out.

In the weeks and months that followed, I was couldn't eat or concentrate in my classes. At night, I couldn't sleep, tossing and turning with images of Nazia, my first friend, my sister, my blood relative, dying in a car crash. *Why didn't I call her back?* I thought. *Why did I delete that message?* At least we could have made up before she left this world. Even worse, why had I let our parents' disagreement affect us? The whole argument seemed so stupid to me, but she was gone and I couldn't tell her that. The fact that she died thinking I hated her filled me with so much guilt and shame. *Maybe she wouldn't have died if we'd spoken,* I thought often.

I felt self-conscious whenever I ran into Nazia's friends, feeling like everyone knew that I didn't call her back. I felt like they were talking about me. Of course, now I realize that very few people were aware that she was trying to contact me, but back then it was all part of the torture I was inflicting on myself. Night after night I couldn't sleep, haunted by the idea that Nazia died without us making up.

Unfortunately, at that time I was so introverted that I couldn't share my deeply disturbing emotions with anyone around me. Who would understand? Also, I was angry with my parents because it was their fault that Nazia and I had drifted apart. During the day, I could avoid these horrible feelings by busying myself with school and social plans. But at night, alone in my room, they bubbled up, almost strangling me with their intensity. I felt so scared lying there in the darkness and then became paranoid because I couldn't sleep. Perhaps if I had told someone how afraid and guilty I felt, they could have helped me see that Nazia's death wasn't my fault. But I couldn't share this with anyone.

One day, I smoked marijuana with my friends and discovered that it helped to calm my nerves and sleep at night. After that, I started smoking pot daily. I was convinced I couldn't sleep without it and that somehow it helped me cope. Or I thought it did.

I never found out the details of Nazia's accident. I didn't need or want to know because what I did know had left me traumatized. And I'm convinced it was one thing that triggered my illness. I was disturbed and at the same time I wasn't talking about this to anybody. That was when I decided to rush to finish my undergrad.

Chapter 8

In Over My Head

"Take it slow
It'll work itself out fine
All we need is just a little patience."
-   *Guns n' Roses*

Shocked by this unexpected tragedy, I dealt with the emotions I couldn't express by immersing myself in my studies. Up until this point, my life was relaxed and easy. I hadn't attended many classes in college and instead was going out with my friends and experimenting with life. I felt no rush to finish school like my peers who had the pressure to graduate so that they could get jobs or apply to graduate school. I didn't need to do either of those things because I came from a privileged family. Money was no object and finances were something I didn't have to worry about.

But after Nazia died, I decided that I had to finish college in a hurry. I had seventeen courses left and knew that if I was busy with that huge workload, I would have no time to think of anything else. This way the tragedy I had just experienced would get pushed out of my mind – or so I thought. So I took seventeen courses in one year and three months. The normal course load would be to do this in two years. I also wanted to excel in subjects that I had never taken before and felt that if my friends could do it, so could I. I put pressure on myself to finish all 400 level courses and two 500 level courses, levels I didn't have to take.

This was a crazy decision for anyone, but even more so for someone with my difficult history in school.

From a very young age, I found school extremely challenging. It was difficult for me to read anything. Whether it was worksheets, a textbook or a novel, I couldn't comprehend the words dancing on the page in front of me. I would read a paragraph over and over and not understand a thing, as if it were almost another language. I couldn't connect phrases and transform their significance in my brain to something meaningful. Even though I tried to follow the lecture, keeping up with the teacher was dizzying and I found it very difficult to understand. It was even harder to write down what I had just heard, making it totally impossible for me to take notes. Instead, I would sit in class and observe. I was always interested in how other people acted so I watched my teachers and the other students with fascination. Of course this didn't help me academically and neither did the fact that I never actually studied. The result was far from satisfactory. My grades were poor.

A few of my teachers would often call my parents, telling them I wasn't doing any work, I wasn't taking notes or that I was a bad student. Other teachers would punish me by making me stand during the entire class or they'd throw me out of the room altogether and make me sit in the hallway. For some reason, I wasn't ashamed of this. At the time, which was from around grade 1 through grade 5, I was very quiet. I didn't make many friends, because I didn't need to. All my girl cousins went to school with me. I had lunch with them and played with them at recess. Why would I need anyone else? But because I was quiet and frequently getting punished, other kids thought I was dumb. I'm not really sure why but I actually liked this because they didn't know who I really was inside. As for my poor grades, I just accepted that I was an average student or "mediocre," which was how my teachers and mother described me.

Even though I was scared when my parents would come talk to me after a phone call with a teacher, I wasn't bothered by my poor grades. I accepted my inability to do school work as part of me and had no intention of doing any better. Starting in grade 1, I had tutors, which is actually very common in our culture because it's so inexpensive. In fact, back when I lived in the big house with my fourteen cousins, we all had tutors. But that wasn't enough for my mother who was unhappy with my performance in school. Actually, both of my parents were. (Looking back now, it seems funny that my education was very important to my parents, although they didn't plan on me actually using it one day.) My mother did not have high expectations from me, but she wanted to help so she would teach me herself afterschool for two hours several days a week. I didn't understand what she was trying to teach me and she was so strict. It didn't feel like help. It felt like she was just interfering in my life. Also, her pushing me to study just made me want to rebel. Sometimes when I'd take a test, I'd hear my parents or teachers telling me how "bad" I was at this or that and then do horribly.

For some reason, my status as a mediocre student and struggling to understand my school work didn't affect my confidence. At that time I didn't think anything was wrong with me or that I had any kind of disability, especially because learning issues weren't as well known as they are today. I simply thought I had to study to do better. Though I never did study, somehow I found my way and passed all my classes while doing or understanding very little.

However, when I was in grade 8, I did so badly on my final exams that I nearly failed. Actually, I did fail math and one other class although I can't remember which one. The school did me a very special favor by promoting me and that wasn't lost on me. This was when something inside me changed. For the first time in my life, I realized I had to do well in school. I was in grade 9 and knew that my board exam was coming up in grade 10. This is the Secondary School Certificate Exam (SSCE) that is taken by grade 10 students all over the country. That's the first serious exam in everybody's life. Finally, I told myself I had to study. During that time, I still had tutors, but my mother stopped interfering in my schoolwork. Without her nagging and constant criticism, I actually became more responsible and began to care about my education. I've seen this in other areas of my life as I've gotten older: any interference affects my performance and my ability to make decisions. If someone tells me "do this" or "do that," I stop functioning.

Now without my mother's interference, I started putting in some effort. I never put in 100%; it was more like 40%. However, that was 40% more than I ever had. I still couldn't read, concentrate in class or take notes. I still couldn't understand what the teacher was saying. But even though something was clearly lacking in me, I never wondered what was wrong with me or thought, "Why can't I take notes?" I didn't get upset or frustrated. Instead, I used to laugh at myself and simply found ways to survive. I knew my friends were there for me and I had enough confidence to ask for help. Instead of seeing it as a problem, I figured out strategies to get around my learning issues. One on one communication was always better for me than being in a class of too many people because I would get distracted. So I made sure I had good friends who would help me with my lessons in class, summarize the lectures and briefly explain what was being taught. I remember one time when I had a big test on a book we were reading and I had no clue what was going on. The exam was 4 o'clock in the afternoon so that morning I asked one of my friends to explain the information to me. I actually got a better grade than she did! The most important favor was that I was allowed to copy my friends' notes.

During that time, I actually discovered that I was quite good at math. Also, to everyone's surprise, especially my own, I did very well on my grade 10 board exam. The school announced those results in front of the whole class and I was stunned when they announced my name *and* said I got one of the top five highest scores. Everyone was cheering for me. I got more attention than the four people who had scored even higher than I had! It was an amazing feeling. Also, I, along with just one other girl, were the only two in a class of 62 people who scored above an 80 on the math.

It wasn't until I was an adult, at 33-years-old, that I learned I had a serious learning disorder. (But I'll share more on that later.) Looking back I don't know how I survived, without understanding a word that my teachers were saying and not being able to take notes.

These learning issues were just some of the reasons taking those seventeen courses in college was a bad idea. Though education was important to my parents, they didn't understand how the system worked in college so they didn't know the immense workload I had taken on. My friends didn't know that I was rushing to finish school either.

"Why did you do that? Why were you in such a hurry?" a friend asked recently.

"Because *you* were finishing your undergrad, so I felt like I had to finish at the same time," I said.

It was during this time that my inability to read started affecting me. I didn't understand anything that I was studying or what my professors were saying. Before that, I'd always been able to get by and even though I wasn't a top student, I had confidence. But now I started comparing myself to friends who were finishing their courses on time. I was trying to compete with peers who were very smart in studies and I was always calculating what grade I needed to have in each course to pass.

Also, for the first time, it struck me: *What am I going to do with my life?*

The pressure was intense and I was anxious all the time.

To this day, I have no clue what I wrote on any of my tests or in my schoolwork and no idea how I survived. Although this struggle was so great and my anxiety so deep, I never talked about this with my friends and parents. It was another emotional battle that I stuffed inside – and one that I think came out in the form of my bipolar illness later on. By the time I graduated, I had a 2.83 GPA. I did not flunk, but I felt like the stupidest person on earth.

Chapter 9

An Uncertain Future

"Every year is getting shorter
never seem to find the time.
Plans that either come to naught
or half a page of scribbled lines."
- Pink Floyd

Although I had worked hard to finish my courses and passed them in record time, the pressures of college life and Nazia's tragic death had dampened my heightened spirits. I felt the anxiety that was bottled within coming to the brim. The end of college life was an important milestone. But rather than thinking about what I'd accomplished and being proud of it, I was fixated on the uncertainty of my future. It was daunting. Even worse, my peers were excited about the road ahead after graduation. They were setting goals of jobs or graduate school. They couldn't wait to fulfill their dreams, while I had no dreams to fulfill. When I thought about my future, it seemed empty and uncertain. I had no direction to take.

I was now at a cross road in my life and the set up of my culture presented me with three options: get married, get a job or pursue higher studies. Since I come from a very privileged background, my life was set for me financially. From a very young age, I knew that I didn't have to worry about what I was going to do when I grew up because I didn't need to earn a living. Yes, education was very important to my parents as was getting a college degree, but they didn't have any expectations about what I should *do* with that education. That was how we were raised – especially the girls in my family. I remember when one of my female cousins graduated from high school. She was getting ready for college and told her father, "I want to teach in a school."

"I'll buy a school for you," my uncle replied. We used to laugh about that, but the uncertainty that this kind of upbringing brought was frightening to me. My whole life what I was supposed to do was all set out for me. After grade one, I would go to grade two. After grade two, I would go to grade three and so on until high school and then college. But *then* what?

Having a career was out of the question. I was not brought up for a 9 to 5 job and wasn't raised to ever think about working. All my male cousins and my brother were encouraged to go into the family business, but no female, no matter how smart she was or how driven, could join them. It was just the way it was.

Although many of my peers were getting married, I knew that marriage was out of the question for me. I felt too young to get married and had no desire to be tied down in a committed relationship. In our culture, your parents set you up with your future husband. Ever since I was 20, my parents were looking for men for me, but I was quite rebellious and refused them all. Luckily, my parents respected that I wasn't ready for marriage.

The easiest option I had was to compete with some of my friends who were going to graduate school. They were very excited about their future in higher studies; for me, it was a way to escape the fear of the unknown. I had no idea what to do with myself or with my life, so I decided to take this route. Although I didn't understand a lot of what my teachers were saying or the work in high school or college, I survived. Back then I never compared myself to my friends. In fact, they always helped me get by. I remember being on the phone with one friend before our board exams in high school and she was saying, "Turn to this page and underline this line." Once I had that information, I did very well.

But now I started comparing myself to other people, friends who were really smart and accomplished. Since they were going for their master's degrees I thought that was the ultimate smartest thing to do. I wanted to be one of them.

Unfortunately, I had no idea how unprepared I was. I enrolled in a GRE course just because there seemed nothing else worth doing. The result was a disaster. Early on in the course, I realized that I was not equipped, mentally or academically to keep up with the demands of the studies. I read the books over and over again, but I could not comprehend most of what I read and nothing seemed to make sense. I was trying to compete with very intelligent and qualified friends doing their GRE. Many of them would do practice papers and tests, but I did not understand the subjects very well and thought that it was not necessary to practice.

Whatever effort I *did* make was clearly not enough. I attempted the first set of exams and walked out of them not understanding the questions. The exam included reading, listening and taking notes and all of this was very challenging for me. I simply had not been able to concentrate or connect to the curriculum and the results were disastrous. I had failed my GRE. I felt like a total idiot and it confirmed that something was terribly wrong with me.

My self-esteem and my spirits took a further downward turn. *Did I learn ANYTHING at university?* I wondered. I had passed through seventeen courses, hard courses at that, but my brain hadn't registered one single thing.

I started feeling confused and disoriented, not being able to understand what was wrong with me. At night, I was unable to sleep and would lie awake battling insomnia. This would leave me in a daze the next day. Soon, each day that passed seemed to blend into the other and I began loosing track of time.

Once again, I started smoking pot to help me fall asleep. Then I began smoking it more and more as this was the only source of relief I had found for myself. It seemed to calm me because I was unable to share my uncomfortable feelings with anyone. No one seemed to notice the pain and suffering I was going through and I had no idea how to let people around me know the kind of loneliness and fear that was welling within. I was very disturbed, but had no one to turn to. I went on with life mechanically, doing things that I was used to doing But the emptiness within started to grow bigger and bigger.

Even when I was at the lowest, I was unable to reach out for help. No one had noticed my pain and no one asked. I did not want to trouble others with my thoughts. I seemed to be plunging into darkness, feeling completely lost and without direction and did not know how to save myself from this hole I found myself falling into.

My anxiety about my future left me hopeless. I am certain that this was the breaking point, the final fissure in my psyche that led to my breakdown and my first hospitalization.

Chapter 10
I Still Haven't Found What I'm Looking For

"Ticking away the moments that make up a dull day
Fritter and waste the hours in an off-hand way
Kicking around on a piece of ground in your home town
Waiting for someone or something to show you the way."
- Pink Floyd

After my disastrous trip to Dhaka for my convocation in 1998, I went back to New York for six months. Then, the following June I returned home. This time, I was much better than before. When I was with friends, I could interact, the frozen tree trunk was starting to thaw. Very slowly and gradually, I began to feel more like myself. I was more independent and my parents were letting go a bit, trusting that I was getting back to myself. Of course, the main reason for this change was the medication. Before I left New York, my doctors had finally figured out the proper medications, the combination and the dose, that I needed to take daily to even the waves that were my moods and emotions.

Even though rationally, I knew the medication was helping, I also was convinced that it made it difficult to concentrate and left my mind blank. A month after I got home, I decided that I was better. I was cured. The old me was back and tired of taking pills. *I'm completely in control now,* I thought. *So why am I taking medication?* Thinking that I knew better and without consulting my doctor or telling my parents, I made the detrimental decision to stop taking my medication. I later learned that this is dangerous for many reasons – one being that if you are going to stop or change medications, you need to do so very slowly and taper off. I also learned that it is very common for bipolar patients to think they're "cured" and stop taking their medication on their own. A month went by and as far as I was concerned, I didn't have any symptoms of my illness. I was fine.

In August, my mother and I travelled to Bangkok and Thailand together for vacation. Anticipating that my mother might ask me where my medication was, I filled one of those pill boxes – the ones that have seven slots, one for each day of the week – with an array of multivitamins. When my mother said, "Where's your medication?" I pulled the vitamin box from the drawer and showed it to her. She was satisfied.

Not surprisingly, my conditioned worsened. Soon, I had a relapse. I became completely manic. I felt happy and as I've said before being in a manic state is actually fun. Well, for the person *in* that state. Not those around her. My mother sensed something was wrong on a trip just the two of us took to New York. We were in the car on the way to our apartment in Long Island from JFK. I don't remember the exact conversation; I just remember that we started arguing. I think it had something to do with how I had acted on the plane. I wasn't manic, but I was very friendly, talking to anyone and everyone around me - even the pilots. For some reason, I went into the cockpit and the pilots let me sit with them for half of the ride from Dhaka to Brussels! They were very nice to me although I do remember a flight attendant going out and asking my mother if I was okay. Clearly, this flight was overwhelming for my mother and is probably how the argument started.

"You know what? I stopped taking my medication," I yelled. "I don't need it anymore!" Then I rolled down the car window and threw my bottle of pills on the street. "I'm not going to take it."

Although she insisted that I needed it, I became very angry and aggressive, telling her that I was fine.

"Trust me," I said. But my mother knew better than that. She had been down this road with me before

Once again, she brought me to the hospital. But this time, she called an ambulance because I aggressively refused to go. When we got to the hospital, they admitted me immediately. The only thing that was the same about the first and second time I was hospitalized was that I was at Cornell. Besides that, it was a totally different experience.

It was actually a turning point in my illness. In many ways, I needed those twenty days to change my life.

Although I was in the same hospital, I was in a different wing. I also wasn't depressed. In fact, I was actually happy and quite confident. The first time I had felt so alone. I didn't talk to anyone and only interacted with others when I *absolutely* had to. This second time, I was quite popular and made many friends. There were about six or seven of us who used to eat meals together and then hang out, talking for hours. I don't remember exactly what we talked about, but I do remember how pleasant it was. Rather than sit alone in my room for endless hours, I socialized, playing checkers and ping-pong with the other patients and sitting in the common area watching the US Open.

I would also talk to the patients who were completely alone. These were the people who never spoke to anybody – the people who were just like I was the first time I had been hospitalized. When I was in school or college and there was someone new, unpopular or quiet I used to make a lot of effort with them. I always wanted other people to feel comfortable and included.

I can't really tell you why the second hospitalization was different, it just was. Some of it was probably due to the medication I was taking (although I had been on medication the last time). Some of it was just the mood I was in. I had a sense of being very much in control during that time. Clearly it showed because a lot of the other patients would say things like, "I don't understand why are you here. You're absolutely fine" or "What are you doing here?"

The first time, I was in a room by myself and would have been miserable if I had a roommate. This time, I shared one with Lisa, an American girl my age who had graduated from NYU, was married and worked for some large financial institution. We got along pretty well.

I also went to group therapy. The first time I was hospitalized I hated group therapy, thinking it was very childish. I went once and never returned. But this time I enjoyed it. I saw that people from all walks of life had issues, many very similar to my own. At night there was a group of about ten or twelve of us who would hang out after therapy and just talk for long hours.

It also helped when I saw other people taking medication. Here were smart and functioning people taking pills, too. They were out in the world doing great things with full and busy days, but they needed medication for the rest of their lives, too. This was a turning-point.

Although the second stay was a happy one, at the same time I was very angry with my parents for putting me in the hospital again. I made unrealistic plans of breaking free from them and making a life of my own as soon as I was out of the hospital. I began dreaming: I would move out of my parents house, get a job in New York City and support myself. The idea made me feel strong and in control, but in reality this dream wasn't feasible. I had no means of supporting myself outside the protected environment of the hospital. I did not have the mental stability to get a decent job nor was I trained to earn my own living. I had not grown up believing that I could and should have a career. I liked the idea of being on my own, but was completely dependent on my family financially and had a mentally unsound and unstable situation. Though it was painful to finally accept the truth, I realized that I was in fact lucky that my parents were supporting me. I would otherwise have been in real trouble.

When I was released from the hospital twenty days later and went to our home Long Island, I felt a sense of emptiness. Maybe that apartment reminded me of the first time I had been hospitalized or maybe it was just getting back to reality. In the hospital I had a group of friends to hang out with, people who were in a similar situation as I was and who understood. It was a safe, controlled environment so facing real life was a stark contrast.

One thing that really helped was an outpatient group therapy I went to four days a week for several hours at a time. There, a group of us met with three instructors. Sometimes we'd all talk together; other times we'd break up into smaller groups with just one of the instructors. We would discuss our lives and our struggles. This was the first time that I talked to other people – strangers, no less – about the deeply painful subject of my illness. I opened up to them as if they were old found friends.

Every time we got together, I'd look around the group amazed at the mix of people, both young and old from all walks of life. There was an NYU student who was clearly very bright and well-read. Then there was a professor from Columbia University who was probably in his early 50's and a businessman who ran a huge, well-known corporation. There were other

61

people too. Some in college, some had graduated from top universities and others had prestigious careers.

At one of the first meetings the girl from NYU, a very pretty girl with thick, shiny hair and dark eyes, spoke.

"I'm going to meet a few of my friends tomorrow and I'm really worried," she said, nervously folding and refolding a small square of paper. "I don't know what to talk about so I've been reading the newspaper so I have topics."

I was stunned. I had seen this girl for several days around the hospital and every time I saw her I thought she was one of the most confident people. Clearly, she was intelligent and yet she was worried about making small talk and sounding stupid. I knew exactly what she was talking about. I had been there.

Then another woman spoke. She was probably in her mid-thirties and had a big job at an advertising agency. "My insurance covers this hospital stay, but if my job finds out that I have this kind of depression, they may discriminate against me," she said. "They may think I'm not competent."

Each session was just like this with all these people revealing what they felt inside. The people were so different from me and yet their emotions and fears mirrored mine. If I had seen any of them on the street, I'd never imagine that they were going through a mental illness. For lack of a better word they seemed so "normal."

Through them, I realized that there were actually other people – successful, bright people - who suffered from the same illness that I did, one that pulled them away from their everyday lives. They showed me that being bipolar isn't something to be ashamed of. It wasn't something that I did wrong, it wasn't something I chose and it wasn't a reflection of me. It was part of me, yes, but it didn't define me. For the first time I realized I was not alone. I was not the only person in the world who had this illness. The weight off my shoulders was tremendous.

Some of us became friends and would go out for coffee after the group therapy or make plans to hang out. We'd been through something together and we all wanted to keep in touch. Except for a girl who I'll call Holly. One day I saw her in the elevator after going to see my doctor. I was about to say hello, when it was clear that she did not want to acknowledge me. She was with three friends. It was strange but I understood completely.

Chapter 11
Give Peace A Chance

"And when the night is cloudy
There is still a light that shines on me
Shine on until tomorrow, let it be."
- The Beatles

My whole life, I have never been driven by my emotions. I have been driven by logic. Getting married is a good example of this. I did not marry my husband out of love; I did so because it was time to get married.

After coming back from New York, life continued to be pretty stable. A year went by without any dramatic incidents. And then a second year went by in the same manner. My highs and lows were pretty much under control thanks to the medication I was taking called Depakote. I decided that it was time for me to get married.

After all, I was twenty-six, an age that would allow me to have healthy kids and if I wanted to share my life with someone, I thought, *Why not start now*?

The previous two years had been the most stable since I could recall and I saw no harm in going ahead with a new experience. In fact, it was going to be a personal challenge and I like a challenge. A doctor or two in the past had warned me against marriage and having a family of my own. I distinctly remember one doctor who I'll call Dr. D. We were talking about any relationships I'd had.

"Well," she said, pausing just a beat too long to irritate me. "About 90% of marriages where one partner suffers from bipolar disorder fail."

I was horrified. And furious.

"And having kids isn't such a great idea either because your children would be genetically vulnerable to this disease," she added. *What the hell are you talking about?* I thought. I was human, too, and had every right to live the life of a normal person. I was not going to let one doctor's opinion hold me back.

Around that time, I was sitting with my father talking.

"Nadera, you're just 26 now," he said. "That's a good age to get married." I didn't say anything, but I agreed.

In my culture, most marriages are arranged when a girl is around the age of 22 or 23, many of these girls not finishing their college education as a result. But when I was that age, I knew that I wasn't ready to find someone who I'd spend the rest of my life with. I was never one of those people who had been dreaming about her wedding day since she was a little girl. In fact, for a long time I didn't think of myself as marriage material. So when my parents tried to set me up with men, I had no interest. Luckily, they accepted this and never pushed me to get married or made me feel rushed to meet someone. That said, I knew my parents had been thinking about my marriage prospects for years and they were thrilled that the subject was finally on *my* mind.

Today, more women find and choose their own partners – that option is always there, but arranged marriages are part of our culture and I was fine with that. Generations ago, arranged marriages meant using the equivalent of professional matchmakers. But today that isn't how people meet someone –

at least not in my social circle. Most of the time it's more word-of-mouth matchmaking, such as your parents have a friend who knows somebody who has a son, cousin, nephew, neighbor, who knows someone. Then they plan for the two of you to meet – sometimes you are aware of this planned meeting; sometimes you're not.

For example, a few years ago my cousin, who is eight or nine years younger than me, was single and of the age to get married. My sister-in-law's best friend was a really nice guy and every time I saw him, I thought of my cousin. So finally I told my sister-in-law that we should have them both come to my house. The day of the meeting, my cousin was at my house and my sister-in-law came over with her friend. At first they were shy with each other, but then I suggested we move to the TV room. Of course, about ten minutes later I made an excuse leave and let them talk privately. Today, they're married and they have three children. That kind of "matchmaking" is common.

Other times it's arranged that a boy and girl meet in some public place like a mall or park, but neither of them has any idea what is going on. Or suddenly a friend or acquaintance will just randomly stop by a girl's home unannounced with a boy. That also happened to me when a neighbor who I rarely ever talked to came to our house with one of her friend's sons. When my mother answered the door, this neighbor spent a few minutes making small talk. But then all of a sudden she asked where I was and if she could see me.

It's funny because I am actually somewhat of a rebel and not traditional so you'd think this type of "arranged" marriage would be just the thing I'd resist. But when it came to choosing men on my own, I didn't have a good track record. I always went for the wrong guy and my relationships never lasted longer than three or four months. None of them were fulfilling and I had no clue what it meant to be in a real relationship. So I was very happy to let my parents find men for me to meet. I had met a couple of guys before at places like the shopping mall unaware that I was supposed to be meeting them, but I didn't like any of them. Then, my parents told me about a relative of a family friend named Abeed and asked if I wanted to meet him. I agreed. (This was the first time I knew in advance that I was going to be introduced to a guy.)

The plan was to meet at this family friend's house at 5 PM. Knowing that I'm a very punctual person, my friend called my mother.

"Nadera can not get to my house before Abeed does so tell her to be a little late," she said. So he came at 5 PM and I arrived at 5:30 PM.

When I walked into the living room, he was sitting on a large, plump couch and stood up to greet me. He was wearing jeans, a gray shirt and a silver watch. At first I was a little uncomfortable. After all, I was in a house I'd never been to before sitting with a man who was a total stranger. I didn't know the family friend very well either. Then after about fifteen awkward minutes, the friend made an excuse to leave the room and we were finally alone. At that moment, I felt like I could stop holding my breath and once we started talking, I was totally at ease. For the next two hours, Abeed and I talked about everything from music to movies. It was nothing serious, but I liked him. For me, the hours seemed to fly by. But not for my mother or Abeed's father who were eagerly awaiting feedback from this meeting. During that time, my mother called her friend almost ten times and Abeed's father called his friend, her husband, even more often.

By then, a great deal of the confidence I had lost from my illness had returned. Still, I was acutely aware that just a year earlier, I wouldn't have

67

been able to carry on this kind of conversation. I wasn't completely back to the girl I was before that September day and still had moments of feeling like I was going to say something stupid, but clearly I was in much better shape.

After that day, Abeed and I started talking on the phone for hours at a time and seeing each other almost every day, going out to lunch or dinner. Talking about music, books, his work, his friends and his family gave me some of idea about the kind of person he was and I could connect with him. My instincts told me that he was "the one." By this, I don't mean that it was love at first sight, because I don't believe in that. I just knew he was a good person and thought he would be for me. This was over the course of three or four months, which drove my parents crazy.

"What is the point of going around all the time and not making a decision?" they would say. But we were taking it slowly. That was important to me.

During one of those long talks, Abeed asked me to marry him. It was late at night, close to midnight and we were on the phone.

"We should get married," he said nervously. Honestly, it was probably the worst marriage proposal ever – so much so that I actually said, "What kind of proposal was that?" I also didn't say "yes." Instead, I told him about my illness.

"You should know something," I said. "I have this illness called bipolar disorder and I have to take medication for the rest of my life."

"I don't care," he said, even though I don't think he'd ever heard of this illness. Although some people may have thought revealing this deeply personal detail would scare him away, I wasn't going to start a life with someone that was based on lies. My instincts told me that he would understand. I felt comfortable sharing my fears and hopes with him and he was quite open and accepting of this. I thought it was unusual that he so easily accepted the fact that I had a psychological illness and knowing that gave me additional courage and strength to go though the marriage plans.

"That's fine," he said.

When I hung up the phone I didn't tell my parents right away. Instead, the next day I went to my uncle's house (my mom's brother's house) to see my aunt and cousins whom I was very close to. They were asking all sorts of questions about Abeed and I said, "I don't have a problem getting married to this guy." Within minutes, my aunt had called my parents and said that I was ready to get married. She was thrilled and so was my father.

Then I had to go to New York for a month. While I was there, Abeed's father went to my father's house to discuss the marriage. Then, they picked a wedding date.

It was a relief to me that my father liked both Abeed and his father. Though I was very rebellious, when it came to making such a huge decision I wanted my parents input and was happy that they were involved and approved. I respected their opinion. I wasn't in love with Abeed at the time. I'm too logical for that. It was more like, *It's time to get married so I'm going to get married.* I did not marry my husband out of love. Yes, I liked him, but it was more that it was time I get married.

Clearly, I was in the best state of mind at this point than I had been since my illness. I wouldn't say the "old" me was back 100%, but I was getting there. I was able to socialize, to enjoy the four ritual parties (today there are 10 or 12!) and the wedding, which in our culture lasts a couple of weeks. All my friends had been very worried and stressed out when they were getting married and planning their weddings, but I was totally calm and relaxed. In fact, I really enjoyed myself. I remember my friends saying things like, "I've never seen a bride as calm as you!"

Abeed and I officially got married on Nov 16, 2000 in a huge wedding. At least 1000 people came. Before the wedding, I was living at home with my parents. Sometimes Abeed would come over and stay at my place. Initially, I was embarrassed to have him sleep in my room. The first time, I told my mom, "He wants to go to my room!"

"Of course," she said. "He's your husband now." Then she said this mantra that in Islam is called TK and does what.

"Okay, you can go to your room," she said when she was finished. It was very funny. But even after that, I felt embarrassed. At about 2 a.m. of the first night Abeed slept over, I felt so weird about it that I threw him out of the house. I literally made him go home in the middle of the night. My parents couldn't believe it when they woke up and he was gone. All in all, the time of my engagement and wedding was very happy and relaxing.

However, married life was different.

At the time I got married, it was common for girls to live with their husband's families. It was just part of our culture. This is what my parents did when they got married and what my brother did with his wife. (Today, this has changed somewhat. More and more young people seem to be getting their own apartments, away from family.) Before I got married, I knew I would live with my Abeed's family, but I didn't think about what it would be like. I guess I thought I would move seamlessly out of the home I had lived in with my parents into my husband's family home. But I was wrong.

It was anything but a seamless transition.

I went from the comfort of my small family of three to living with practical strangers. This included my father-in-law, two sister-in-laws, and

70

one brother-in-law and his wife. (Abeed's mother had died about a year before we were introduced so I had never met her.) One of Abeed's sisters was just 13-years-old and, without a mother, she still needed a lot of care and attention.

We all lived in one very big house and although we were in separate apartments, my in-laws were just across the hall. In my family, my parents always respected my privacy and our home was large enough that I always had plenty of space and time to myself. But it wasn't like this in my in-laws' home. They would come over to our apartment unannounced, which felt like a huge invasion of privacy. Abeed's teenage sister would walk in whenever she wanted "just to say hi" and his father would come by, sit down on the couch and watch TV. We also ate all our meals together. This was too much interaction for me. I'm a very free spirit, independent and someone who likes my privacy so I found life with Abeed's family very suffocating. Simple things were stressful. They'd get upset if we went out do dinner and didn't tell them and I felt like I had to let them know when I left the house during the day. It felt like I was restricted and that there was an invasion of my privacy. I never imagined married life like that.

My in-laws were also different from my family in terms of their values and background. They were brought up differently than I was and I found some of their habits and family rituals strange. Nothing was planned or organized. They didn't talk much or smile. And my father-in-law was always irritated. I had always prided myself on being able to get along with anyone, yet this was different. I thought of them all like aliens and didn't know how to handle them. With friends, you may have differences or qualities you don't like, but you can overlook them because you don't actually have to live with those differences.

As a new bride, I really wanted Abeed's family to like me and put a huge amount of pressure on myself to impress them and please them. They, too, had a lot of expectations of me and were adjusting to someone new moving into their family. I used to do a lot for them, not because Abeed asked me to, but because it was what I thought I *should* do. I'd take his youngest sister shopping and to her friends' houses. I'd hang out with his other sister and his brother. For my father-in-law, I'd do errands and TK. Not once did they ever say, "Thank you" or seem appreciative. No matter how hard I tried, I felt like it was a thankless job.

It was hard to adjust to the new circumstances, as it would be for anyone settling into a new environment. Plus, as an only child in a small family, I had never had to compromise. I'd never shared a room or toys or anything. Now, with this new family, compromising was inevitable. This would be difficult for any new bride, but my intense mood swings made the process especially difficult for me. I couldn't handle the stress.

At the time, Abeed and I had a strong relationship and never bickered about personal differences or issues. The only thing we only fought about was his family. I felt that they were rude and unappreciative. He thought I should give them some time.

Shortly after we were married, my brother-in-law got married and he and his wife moved abroad with their family to Hong Kong. Then the older of my two sister-in-laws moved to Australia. Now, the responsibility of my widowed father-in-law and teenage sister-in-law were left to me and Abeed and I was furious. The pressure of this took a toll on my relationship with my husband and I became vulnerable to stronger mood swings than I had ever been in the recent past. I ignored my husband and became totally focused on how not to loose control of my equilibrium.

In March of 2003, Abeed had to go to Bangkok for work and I went with him. I thought it would be good to get away from home, but I was under so much stress that I was tossing and turning every night. Getting enough sleep is critical for my health and without it I started to feel sick. I was not only tired, but irritable and annoyed at the slightest thing. I was also starting to think about having children and the thought of getting pregnant petrified me – everything from what my body would be like, how I'd feel and what it would be like for my entire life to change completely because of a baby. When we returned home from Bangkok, I could just feel that I was having a manic episode.

"I'm getting sick," I told Abeed. "I'm going to my parents house." I took a shower and then he drove me there. My parents had dealt with my illness before. Also, I wasn't that comfortable in our home because we had so many people all around us. At my parents' house, I knew I could have some privacy.

"I'm not feeling well," I said when my mother opened the door. "I feel like I'm going to get sick." Immediately, she called my doctor in Dhaka, Dr. Mirza. He came to their house and gave me sedatives and readjusted my medication.

Besides the lack of sleep, I think my medication was part of why I got sick again. Just six months earlier, I'd talked to my doctor about getting pregnant. I was on Depakote, which you can't be on while pregnant, to lithium, which is known to be safe for pregnancy. Although many people have very good experiences on this medication, it never suited me. It made me feel very drowsy and gave me a lingering sense of anxiety and sadness.

This manic episode was short-lived, lasting only a few days. But despite it's brief duration, it was very significant. It was the first time that

Abeed had seen me in a totally manic state. Yes, he knew about my bipolar disorder before we got married, but there's a huge difference between *knowing* it and actually *seeing* me like that and experiencing it. At one point, I didn't even recognize him, my own husband! He was terrified. And yet, through it all, despite the pain and anguish of this period, Abeed took care of me. He stayed by my side constantly. This meant everything to me.

It was also significant because this episode was the first time my in-laws learned that I was bipolar. They were very kind and respectful and tried to comfort Abeed. They came to see me at my parents' house. I don't know what they saw because I barely remember their visit, but they never criticized me or said anything directly to me about my illness. Instead they gave me exactly what I needed: a lot of support and privacy. They went out of their way to be sensitive to my needs and patiently waited for me to get healthier. This change was the first turning point in our relationship.

But my in-laws weren't the only ones who were changing. I was slowly changing, too, getting my confidence back.

Chapter 12

On My Way Back

"When you feel like hope is gone
Look inside you and be strong
And you'll finally see the truth
That a hero lies in you."
- Mariah Carey

Like I said earlier, after my illness in 1998, I didn't want to mix with any of my old friends because I though they had expectations of me that I couldn't fulfill. I thought they wanted to spend time with the "old" me, the person I was before I was hospitalized and that girl was gone. Instead, I hung out with newer friends and distanced myself from most of the people who knew me before. But gradually my confidence was coming back.

One very clear sign of this for me was before a trip to New York in 2007. TK NAME was a very close friend before my illness. Now, she lived in New York at the time. We had always been great friends and many times since my illness she had reached out to me. She wanted to visit when I was pregnant and after I had my daughter, but I always found excuses not to see her. Other friends also tried to connect with me and I avoided them, too. The "old" me was too much to live up to. I thought I couldn't.

But for some reason, before I left for that New York trip, I called her. I told her I was coming to the States and wanted to make plans. That may sound like a small step, but for me it was enormous, not only in terms of reuniting with my old friends, but to gain my confidence back. My friend took the day off from work and we planned to meet for lunch near her apartment in mid-town Manhattan. I was very nervous to see her. Even though I was conscious of what I was saying, wondering if a remark I made was stupid, I realized that she was not going to judge me. She didn't care about being with the "old" me or the "new" me, she just wanted to be with *me*, whoever I was right now. This motivated me to start connecting with my other friends, too.

Around this time, the owner of the house Abeed's family was renting decided he wanted to move in. We had to find another place to live. I saw this is as a sign, as our chance to break away from the suffocating situation with his family. We chose an apartment building that was far enough from my in-laws that you had to drive to see them. Of the 20 families who were living in that building, I knew all off them. One was actually my best friend Lamiza. It may sound exciting and fun, but I was still on my gradual road to recovery and sometimes too much social interaction was still very uncomfortable for me. I needed my own personal space and dreaded the thought of neighbors dropping by unannounced or being unable to avoid small talk in the elevator or hallway.

"It's too close to too many people we know," I told my husband.

"But it's the best building we can find with an apartment that's exactly what we need," he said. He was right so we me moved anyway. It turns out all that forced socializing was exactly what *I* needed, too.

People did drop by unannounced all the time and I was constantly running into people and having to make small talk. I couldn't avoid seeing neighbors that I knew. In the beginning, all this interaction was challenging and I felt completely out of my comfort zone. I forced myself to smile, chat and be social. But over the three years that we lived there, it became natural. I actually liked being around my neighbors. Soon enough, I was the one encouraging *and* hosting spontaneous get-togethers. Before my illness, I always loved having people around me. I saw myself as a people-person. This new life was a little of the "old" me coming back and it felt great. It was like a club house. During that time, I realized that people weren't judging me. They weren't comparing me to someone they knew almost a decade ago. They just wanted to be with me, the me I was in that moment. No one else.

I loved the three years we lived in that apartment building away from my in-laws. But then Abeed's other sister was moving to Austrailia. She, Abeed and his brother were worried about us not being in the same building as Abeed's father and young sister just in case anything happened to his father. If we lived in separate places and she had to move in with us, it would be too disruptive to her routine.

So built a five-story building for the entire family. But this time instead of being just across the hall from my in-laws, each of our families has a separate floor. My husband, children and I live on two floors and my father-in-law and sister-in-law live one floor below us. My brother-in-law and his family will live on another when they get back from Hong Kong. We all have separate entrances, but at least we're in the same building to help my father-in-law with Abeed's sister.

Life became easier when we moved into these independent flats. Everything changed for the better with my in-laws. We all learned to adjust to one another. The biggest change happened within *me*. I learned to find my voice and realized that I didn't need to try so hard to make them happy. I found ways to have my own space and no one bothered me. I also realized that when I'd first married and moved in with Abeed, his family was still grieving the relatively recent loss of their mother. Often it's a mother that holds the family together, but they had lost this glue. In those early years, my father-in-law was depressed over his wife's recent death and the huge responsibility of caring for his young daughter and other children on his own. I didn't understand that at the time. But as the years healed that loss a bit, my father-in-law transformed, too. I was able to see the person he truly is which is a really smart, engaging man. Later, I also realized that our marriage had been a new experience, not just for me, but for Abeed's family. They had a new person in their house and their family dynamic was changing.

When I look back, I realize that I worried too much and let the little things bother me. I gave this topic so much importance. Now I am completely myself. If I do things for my in-laws, it's because I *want* to not because I feel pressure to impress them. Today, when I make even the smallest gesture, they are so appreciative. They say, "thank you" five times. They are just happy I'm there. They know when I need my space and have accepted the fact that I can be very moody. My in-laws support has been invaluable to me and given me the additional strength to hold our family together. Today, I'm much more calm and cool.

Now we see them about once a week for a meal. Occasionally, my sister-in-law comes for ten or fifteen minutes to ask for something, but then she goes home. I'm her favorite, probably because I know how to deal with her. I don't get angry with her and give her whatever she wants.

I also came to understand how hard it must have been for Abeed to adjust to my mood swings, which at times were very strong. Sometimes Abeed took my mood swings personally. Of course, they have nothing to do with my husband and it can be frustrating for him. Many times, we had misunderstandings and fought violently, yet never once did he attack me personally, saying that he was tired of me or my illness. Even in the midst of an argument or a heated moment, he has never used it against me or said anything mean or hurtful – and I'm sure there are plenty of times that he could have.

Chapter 13
A Life-changing Doctor

"There can be miracles, when you believe
Though hope is frail, it's hard to kill
Who knows what miracles you can achieve
When you believe, somehow you will
You will when you believe."
- Whitney Houston

If you're really lucky, you meet at least one person who truly changes your life. I met that person. But she not only changed my life, she saved it.

Once again, I made another serious but logical decision in my life. I was 29-years-old, had been married three years and, as a result, decided that it was the right time to get pregnant. Like many women, I felt a strong urge to be a mother. But part of my reasoning was because I wanted to be a normal person with a family and kids to care for. I also wanted to defy the various people who told me that I shouldn't have children because of my illness.

One of these nay-sayers was Dr. Churchin, the psychiatrist I saw after the first time I was hospitalized. I don't recall what we were talking about or what prompted it. I just know that it was years before I was even thinking of getting married, let alone having children. But I remember her deeply disturbing words so clearly.

"Bipolar disorder is genetic so there's a strong possibility that your children may have it, too." she said, matter-of-factly. "You might want to adopt one day rather than have a baby of your own,"

I was stunned. *Is it a bad thing to bring someone into the world who is like me?* I was furious. Right then, I knew more than ever that someday I was going to try and have my own child.

So in 2003, when I decided it was the right time to get pregnant, I told my psychiatrist. I was in New York so she suggested I see a doctor at New York Presbyterian Hospital-Weill Cornell Medical Center who specializes in reproductive psychiatry. I had never heard of such a thing but it turns out that this is an area of mental health that helps women deal with various emotional and psychiatric conditions before, during and after pregnancy. Her name was Dr. Catherine Birndorf and she was actually the founding director of the Payne Whitney Women's Program at the hospital.

The plan was that I would still see my regular psychiatrist for therapy sessions, but Dr. Birndorf would manage my medicine before and during my pregnancy. At the time, I wasn't a computer person so I had my friend Radeeya email Dr. Birndorf to make an appointment. Dr. Birndorf suggested we book a double session – almost two hours - so I could fill her in on my health history, my life etc.

I thought I was meeting with yet another doctor. What I didn't realize was that those two hours would change my life profoundly.

On November 21, 2002, Abeed and I arrived at Dr. Birndorf's office for the appointment. But she wasn't there. I waited and waited, getting more annoyed as the minutes passed. I am a very punctual person so the more I waited, the more restless I became, pacing up and down the corridor, wondering whether I had made the right decision to meet with her. Abeed tried to calm me down, but I was agitated and annoyed. Twenty minutes later, I was furious. We were about to leave when I saw a woman rushing down the hallway towards me.

"I'm Dr. Birndorf," she said breathless but smiling. My first thought was that she was very casually dressed for a doctor wearing beige slacks and a white shirt with her hair pulled back loosely into a ponytail. Something about her felt right and my anger disappeared. I felt instantly calmed. It sounds strange to say about a therapist, but it was love at first sight.

Dr. Birndorf did not have the air of a typical psychiatrist and once I sat down, an amazing feeling of connection and comfort washed over me. My instincts told me that I could trust her. She wasn't stuck up like the other psychiatrists I had met over the last five years and she didn't keep her distance. She was warm and kind and open. She also knew a lot about my culture because she had been to this part of the world. There was something unconventional about her. If I went to a session and she said, "How are you?" I could ask, "What about you?" Any doctor I'd seen before made it clear that I couldn't ask them anything about themselves. To them this was professional; to me it made the connection even more distanced. It didn't work.

I know that not every patient asks Dr. Birndorf those kinds of questions or cares to. But for me it was different. I was revealing myself to her so I wanted to know about her life. Where did she grow up? Was she married? How many children did she have? The fact that she didn't mind these queries spoke volumes to me. Relationships with any other doctor had felt formal and strained. This was as comfortable as sitting with an old friend. And yet I also felt like Dr. Birndorf could take care of me, that she could really help me.

"When are you coming to Bangladesh?" I asked her at one of our first meetings. "I need you." She smiled.

With Dr. Birndorf, I didn't *have* to see her I wanted to see her. I looked forward to it. With other doctors, I didn't want to talk or open up and when I did they just seemed to be listening. Dr. Birndorf not only listened to me, but understood what I was talking about. I remembered one session years earlier with a previous psychiatrist. I began the session talking about something very important to me and she looked at me quizzically as if hearing it for the first time.

"I told you about this," I said.

"I don't remember that," she said, shaking her head and shrugging her shoulders as if it was no big deal. I was so annoyed and clearly my expression revealed how upset I was. But instead of being sympathetic she said, "You can't expect me to remember *everything*, do you?"

Aren't I paying you to remember? I thought. I'd never connected with that doctor from day but one, but in that moment I knew this was it. She didn't keep track of what I'd been doing and saying.

Initially, I was seeing both Dr. Birndorf and Dr. Chuchin at the same time, because Dr. Birndorf was supposed to focus on my pregnancy only. At the time, I was on Depakote, a medication that was not recommended during pregnancy so Dr. Birndorf switched me to lithium. Although the latter is safer during pregnancy, it never suited me. It made me feel a little down and sluggish, but I switched because Dr. Birndorf said she had had very good experiences with pregnancy and lithium. When you take lithium, you have your blood drawn once a month to determine if the levels are safe.

I did this whether I was in Bangladesh or NY with Dr. Birndorf monitoring the results.

But after a few months the differences between Dr. Churchin and Dr. Birndorf were too great and my glaring lack of connection to Dr. Churchin stood out even more. It was of no use. My next session, after several months since our first appointment, I told Dr. Birndorf, "I want you to be my regular doctor. I'm very comfortable with you." She said okay. After that, I never went back to Dr. Churchin and I didn't miss her for one single second.

Dr. Bindorf continued counseling me even when I was in Bangladesh via weekly telephone calls from New York. Sometimes our meetings are very regular, other times they haven't been. But despite that, her help has been immeasurable. Over the years, Dr. Bindorf has seen me during very trying and difficult moments in my life, the worst moments of my life. She knows everything about me. Truthfully, she knows more about me than my husband. She has seen everything and has patiently accompanied my personal growth to bring me to where I am today and I've told her a lot of things that I've never shared with anyone in my life. She helped me achieve balance in many ways – literally and figuratively - so that I could be in control of my illness.

One of those was helping me find the right medication. In 2005, I was having problems sleeping for what seemed like no reason. I'd never had a sleeping problem in my whole life so it was really bothering me. I told Dr. Birndorf about this during a phone session one day.

"You should try Quetiapine," she said. Quetiapine, which is a drug used for mental disorders, was a relatively new drug but Dr. Birndorf spoke very highly of it. I took a very small dose of it with the lithium that I was taking at the time and that I had been taking since 2003. It totally worked for me. I felt much calmer and more relaxed and slept really well. She also told me that if I felt a little anxious I could take a little more of it during the day.

Wouldn't it be great if I could take this for my illness instead of lithium? I thought after being on it for a couple of months. At the time, I was seeing a psychiatrist in Bangladesh. But when I asked him about this, he said no. "You can't do that," he said. Shortly after that, I asked Dr. Birndorf the same thing. "Of course you can take it instead," she said. Dr. Birndorf had had good experiences with this drug in her other patients.

I was thrilled! Still, I couldn't immediately go off lithium. Instead, I had to taper so my body would get used to the new medication while the lithium got out of my system. Over the course of a month, I slowly took less and less lithium and more Quetiapine. It was gradual, but once I was totally on the Quetiapine it was life-changing. Lithium had never suited me. I'd only gone it because I was trying to get pregnant. But it always made me feel tired, foggy and sort of sluggish. It also made me feel a little down, sort of unlike myself.

Once I was totally off of it and only on Quetepaine, it was like my view of the world was crystal clear, not foggy. I felt more alert, energetic and calm. In turn, this feeling of being more like the "old" me, of seeing life more clearly, was just another little jolt of confidence on my road to recovery. Another one of those tiny steps that, when added to all the others, was getting me back to an even better version of the "old" me.

Today, after over a decade of on and off counseling, Dr. Birndorf has become more like a friend than my psychiatrist. I never imagined that there could be a doctor like Dr. Birndorf and I don't think there are many like her. But one thing I know for sure: I am convinced that Dr. Birndorf was sent to this world to rescue me when I was sinking. And I know that I could not have stayed a float without her.

Chapter 14

In My Daughter's Eyes

"This miracle God gave to me,
gives me strength when I am weak.
I find reason to believe
In my daughter's eyes."
– Martina McBride

It took me three months to get pregnant and during that time my mood swings were monitored regularly and I kept a close check on any unusual incidents that might have raised any hint of alarm. Thankfully, there were none. My mental health was stable during my pregnancy and I had no issues with my medication. Unfortunately, there were other problems.

When I was 24 weeks pregnant, I flew from Dhaka to New York with my father. The plan was for me to stay in my parents' Long Island apartment and to have my baby in New York because the hospitals are better than they are in Dhaka –especially in case of any emergencies. I was enjoying my time in New York. Then, when I was 28 weeks pregnant, it was mid-February and I was shopping at Bloomingdales with one of my old friends who lived in New Jersey at the time. The whole day I felt a little bit uncomfortable. Something just didn't seem right.

Then, standing between racks of maternity dresses, I realized what was wrong: I could not feel my baby move. Usually, I could feel a little bit of movement, a sense that my baby was growing and living in my stomach. But suddenly, I felt nothing. I was petrified. I dropped the clothing in my hand and sat down on a bench already occupied by a mannequin. Because it was the weekend, I couldn't call my regular doctor directly. Instead, I had to call the hospital, speak to a service and then the on-call doctor would call me back. I left my message with the service and then waited. Twenty minutes later, I was in a taxi going back home to Long Island when that call came.

"I can't feel the baby move," I said to the doctor.

"Go to the hospital," he said. "Right away."

I told the cabdriver to turn around and head back to Manhattan and drop me at Cornell Hospital. There, they admitted me immediately and did an array of tests like stress tests and sonograms, The results revealed that my baby's heartbeat was 220 beats per minute which is very, very high. I was also having contractions. At 28 weeks, this was not good.

I stayed in the hospital overnight while they monitored my contractions and my daughter's heartbeat and told me she had something called an arrhythmia. I wound up staying in the hospital for three or four days while they monitored me and had me on an IV. I couldn't eat or drink anything for 24 hours. This was really unfortunate for me since I was craving a Coca Cola – which I was not supposed to have even when I *could* eat because I couldn't have caffeine, among other things like salt. Every time the doctor came to check on me, I begged her for a Coke.

"Why can't I have one?" I'd ask. After two days, she came into my room and handed me a glistening, red can. A coke!

"Finally," she said. "You can have this." To this day, it was the best Coke that I've ever tasted.

At that time, my husband wasn't in New York yet. This was probably a good thing since he's a nervous kind of guy. I'm much stronger. Even in the hospital during those days when I wasn't sure if my daughter was going to be born early or not, for some reason, I was fine. My father rushed to meet me at the hospital that first day and was crying when he saw me lying on the bed, hooked up to an IV with an oxygen mask over my head. My mother was in London and he called her and told her she had to come to New York right away. He also called my husband. *Why are they coming?* I thought. I was very comfortable without them.

Although it was the same hospital that I had been in twice for mental illness, it didn't remind me much of that time. In fact, I barely thought about it. Perhaps it was because I was in a different wing. But I also think it's because, when it comes to big things, I'm a strong person. Oddly enough, it's the little things in life and small decisions that can tie me up and make me worry. *What should I wear to a party? What should I order from the menu?* Those things stress me out a lot. But in serious situations, I'm fine. I was very calm and remember times when I'd just sit in my hospital room and stare at the East River for hours.

The doctors considered inducing my pregnancy, but decided it was better not to. Instead, they would just monitor me closely. For the next five weeks after I was released from the hospital, I was not bedridden but my activity and food were very severely restricted. I also had to go to the hospital every day - sometimes even on the weekend- so they could do a full ultra-sound and stress tests to monitor the baby. It was a difficult and overwhelming time for me –especially so late in my pregnancy when just carrying that extra weight was exhausting. I wasn't one of those women who enjoyed being pregnant. The extra pounds and my big stomach made me feel clumsy, heavy and unattractive. Now adding this stress made it much worse. I hated having to constantly go to the hospital and I was worried about my daughter. I became very quiet and withdrawn, always worrying if the baby was moving or not. *Was she okay?* I was not myself. I was very down and. That said, although I wasn't myself my parents weren't worried that I was having a manic episode and neither was I. It was just a different feeling.

Finally, my daughter was born at 33 weeks, in May of 2004. She was five pounds, five ounces and I named her Ilham, an Arabic name that means "inspiration." At the time I had no clue how well her name would fit her. Or that she would turn out to change my life and mark the biggest turning point in my recovery from my illness. But that came later.

First, she went immediately from the delivery room to the neonatal intensive care unit (also known as the NICU). There, she was in an incubator and no one was allowed to visit her except my husband and me. Looking back, I can't believe it *didn't* make me more upset to see all those wires attached to Ilham's frail, tiny body and to only be able to watch her in that plastic incubator rather than hold her in my arms. But for some reason I was like a zombie and not feeling much of anything at the time.

After two days, I was released from the hospital but Ilham stayed five more. I did not feel particularly happy or sad at her birth. All the stories I had heard about other mothers being over the moon at the first sight of their newborn baby sounded strange to me. Although I was grateful that Ilham was born healthy but for some heart troubles, I did not sense any "special motherly" feeling. I didn't feel that instant connection people rave about. *What's wrong with me?* I wondered. Ilham had been delivered by c-section so I was also in a lot of pain. People would say, "Don't you want to see your baby?" which made me feel even worse about our lack of connection.

Once Ilham was released, Abeed and I brought her back to my parents' apartment in Long Island. It was horrible. All my life, I had never taken on any serious responsibility or had to care for anything besides myself. Now, I was fully responsible for another human being, a very tiny and dependent human being with basic but constant needs for food, changing and comfort. It was shocking to me. Having your first baby is difficult for many people, no matter the situation but doing so in my parents' small apartment with my mother always hovering was awful. My mother, although helpful, was annoying and her constant nagging gave me so much stress. And although my husband had been there at Ilham's birth and came back and forth a few times, he had to go back home to Dhaka for work.

Another source of stress was the fact that Ilham had a health condition that required special attention all throughout the first year. During that time, she needed to be monitored constantly and had a halter strapped to her tiny body. I had to be very careful with her diet and keep a close watch on her. She needed regular medical visits and medicine four times a day. I attended to this single handedly. I began to grow tired and irritable.

We went back to Bangladesh in July, but things didn't get easier. Yes, caring for her got easier because I had more help in my home. But I didn't feel connected to my beautiful, newborn daughter. This really worried me.

Where's that new mom euphoria everyone talks about? I wondered. *Why isn't it happening to me?*

I was very shaky and worried all the time and I didn't feel confident in how I was caring for my daughter. I certainly didn't feel confident being alone with her. *What is all this bullshit about how great it is to have a baby?*

91

I thought. *I don't get it.* Anybody in this situation has to adjust but for me, because of my illness, everything in life takes even more adjusting. It took me more that a year to connect with my daughter as I struggled with post-partum depression.

It did not happen the way it does in books or movies where there's this instant moment of love and connection. (And thoughts of those books and movies made me feel even worse.) No. For me, it took me a while to get me connected with my daughter. *Where are those magical feelings of love? Where is our connection?* Instead of floating on a cloud of love and excitement, I was a zombie.

What made it worse was that I literally had everything in my life. I had a husband, a child, a beautiful home, loving parents and extended family and financial security- and I wasn't happy. Anybody in my shoes would have been thrilled. But I was miserable. That struck me really hard and made me feel even worse. My misery in the midst of such an amazing life seemed so crazy - even to *me* - so I knew I couldn't tell anyone about these feelings.

Around the same time, my sister-in-law got married and moved with her husband to Hong Kong and my brother-in-law moved to Australia. On top of the post-partum depression I was struggling with and my new responsibilities as a mother, I did not like shouldering the huge responsibility of taking care of my father-in-law and teenage sister-in-law. This made me angry. I felt that this should have been a shared responsibility but now it was up to my husband and I.

Sometimes the pressure was so enormous and unbearable that I sought solace in smoking pot. I thought that it helped calm my nerves and gave me the strength and courage to cope with my life. I didn't tell anyone, not even my husband. In the months that followed, pot became my secret companion.

I knew it was not right. I needed to be more responsible, after all now I was someone's mother. Yet felt I could not relax and get through another day without relaxing my nerves with a bit of the perfumed leaf. I was afraid I was going in the wrong direction, but could not help myself. Each time the pressure grew, I smoked more and more pot. My addictive tendency was getting the better of me and I was now getting very afraid. We need to add more here. This is so interesting and very common.

Before getting pregnant, I had worked very hard to be as healthy as possible, quitting all intoxicants and avoiding cigarettes. Although I knew I had to stop smoking pot for my child, I also knew that I was going through a weak phase and did not have the strength to fight this demon alone.

I am grateful that I found the courage and good sense to turn for medical help before it was too late. Once again, I reached out to Dr. Birndorf. I think we need more of this here did you quit? How? This could really help other women who think they can't quit once they start.

Then one day happened. I went out shopping with my nin-month-old daughter and she fell asleep without eating. I felt so bad that I just started crying and crying. In that moment, my emotions were so strong and deep and my heart was so heavy. I felt like I couldn't possibly care for anybody in the world like I did for her. She was everything to me – a feeling I'd never had before.

As I said earlier, my depression had left me numb and often emotionless for years. I couldn't feel anything even when I wanted to. I couldn't cry at my own grandmother's funeral despite how close I was to her and how much I loved her. But at that moment, watching my sleeping baby daughter and worrying about her well-being, I actually felt *something* and I felt it *strongly*. I was shedding the emotion-less zombie. I wanted to be healthy – all for her. *I want the happy me back*, I thought. *I cannot let my illness take me over*. It wasn't just me anymore. Now, I had someone else relying on me, someone else who was intricately connected to me. *I cannot lead my life with all this anxiety, these negative feelings and fear.* I'm not saying it was easy to do this or it was like I just flipped a switch and changed. No, it was difficult and gradual.

But it was only because of my daughter that I fought my mood swings. The more I took care of her, the more we bonded. I wasn't one of those women who dreamed of motherhood as a little girl or envisioned myself as a mother. But now with every trip to the doctor, every diaper change and every bath, I gained confidence. Although I did not have an instant connection to Ilham when she was born, she became the stick I would lean on to be able to walk straight once again. I am convinced that without her help, I would have smoked my brains to oblivion.

Chapter 15
Reading Disorder

"I am not in competition with anyone else.
I run my own race.
I have no desire to play the game of being better
than everyone else around me
in any way, shape or form.
I just aim to improve, to become a better person than I was.
That's me and I'm free."
– Source Unknown

By now you know that I see Dr. Bindorf as one of the biggest blessings in my life. Without her, I would not be the person I am today. And my life would not be what it is today. She has been my strength when I was weak and with her support, I have been able to live, rather than exist, and face my challenges bravely. She is a huge part of the confidence I gained in many ways.

During my psychotherapy sessions, I would complain to Dr. Birndorf about not being able to understand things. I also told her about my childhood experiences in school, about how I couldn't take notes and how I could never comprehend a word that my teachers were saying. After several years,

Dr. Birndorf knew about all my academic struggles. Then one day, in April of 2007, she stopped me mid-sentence.

"Maybe you have a learning disability," she said. "Have you thought of that?" I shook my head. At the time, I hadn't heard much about learning disabilities.

"You should go get tested," Dr. Birndorf said. She referred me to a TK TYPE of specialist, Dr. Dahlman. I had one appointment just to meet her and then I went through three or four days of various tests and examinations. Some were written, some were on the computer. There was reading, multiple choice and even math.

A few weeks later, Dr. Dahlam had my test results. The plan was for her to give them to me with Dr. Birndorf. It was a hot August day, when I met the two of them at Dr. Birndorf's office. I was very nervous why did you want to be with her when you heard the news.

The results: I had a reading disorder. So it's just reading not more like a learning disability?

As much as this saddened me, the news was a great relief. I finally understood why I had struggled in school and why it had been so hard for me to take notes. I was not stupid after all. There was nothing wrong with my intelligence. It was a big weight off my shoulder.

This discovery gave me additional courage and a new enthusiasm. I had learning disabilities and yet I had *survived*! I had graduated from high school and college despite this serious handicap. I was proud of myself for having come this far in life. It was another little deposit in the bank of my confidence.

So I set myself a new goal: to read a book on my own. This may sound small to you, but for me it was huge. Actually enormous! I had never read a book, a *whole* book, on my own. I had always been fascinated by people who were well-read because for me reading even a paragraph was nearly impossible. But now, I wanted to try. I decided on a book that I already had on my shelf called *Silk* by Caitlin Kieran that was 120 pages long. (Although I never read books, it gave me a lot of satisfaction to be in a library or bookstore and I loved buying books, collecting them the way some people collect souvenirs.)

When I started, I could not even understand the first page, actually I couldn't understand the first paragraph. I read it over and over again. Then, with courage and effort, I went forward, slowly but surely. I was determined. Within 48 hours I had managed to complete this book and understand it, all on my own. You can't imagine what satisfaction I got from that small little book. The feeling was exhilarating. It was as if I had climbed Mount Everest!

That was a pivotal moment that pushed me to want to learn things and know things. I felt like I had lost so many years when I was ill and recovering that I was in a rush to learn more.

Next, I decided to read *The One* by Richard Bach. It was a book someone had given me (I can't remember who) back in 1998 after my illness. I had carried it around with me for almost ten years so I thought it was finally time to actually open it. I ready it day and night, at home and in the car. I didn't put it down because I was determined to finish it. And I did.

That year I read 20 books. And in three years, I read almost 80 books. Even when I read a book I didn't like, I always finished it. I was elated that despite a serious disorder, I could push through that no obstacle could stop me.

One of my favorite books became *Stranger* by Albert Cummings. One line I really love is, "Wherever I will be, I want to remember this life wherever I go." Why does this mean something to you?

Chapter 16
New Beggaring

"God grant us the serenity
to accept the things we cannot change,
courage to change the things we can,
and wisdom to know the difference."
- The Serenity Prayer

In thirteen years of marriage, Abeed and I have had our ups and downs, our good times and our bad. I have not been perfect.

However, despite his committed devotion to me, Abeed has made his mistakes. The biggest was an eight-month affair that happened when I was pregnant with my second child. I didn't find out about the affair until two years after it was over. It's strange because even before I discovered it, my instincts told me that something wasn't exactly right in our marriage. Before my illness, I'd always followed my instinct, but afterwards I had stopped. I guess I no longer trusted myself. After all, if I could lose my mind out of nowhere (or so it seemed to me), how would I know if my instincts were correct?

Over the years, my husband and I grew slightly apart as I was unable to give him the attention he deserved and needed from a spouse. I did not realize this, as I was too focused on myself and struggling with my own highs and lows to be concerned or aware of his emotional and personal needs.

It was 2008 and I was pregnant for the second time. I was thrilled. I was also much calmer and less afraid than I'd been the first time. Around 24 weeks, I decided to go to New York for two months by myself. My daughter was four and a half years old and my mother and Abeed would care for her while I was gone. Although I felt very bad when I left her, I knew she was busy with school and activities and I also knew that I couldn't handle her and my pregnancy at the same time. And since I was going to have my son in New York, I made the choice to spend some extra time alone there.

For me, this was another life-changing moment. It was a very relaxing and freeing time where I could focus only on myself because I had no one else's needs to take care of. Every night I went out for dinner, to the opera or to see a Broadway show. I spent time with friends who lived in New York and also had different friends from all over come to visit for a few days at a time here and there.

At this point, I had my own apartment in Long Island in the same building as my parents' apartment. So even when my father was there for two weeks, I had privacy. During that time, I took very good care of myself, eating well, getting lots of rest and just relaxing rather than worrying. I got to know myself and finally, *finally,* could say I felt happy with myself. This was huge considering the state I'd been in just a few years earlier. It gave me a lot of confidence and, although it had taken a long time, it seemed like the "old" me had fully returned.

I'm not saying that it was all perfect because it wasn't. I had my bad days. Sometimes I felt really, really down in the morning, but I knew how to lift myself out of it. I'd take a shower and force myself to go out with friends, go to a museum or go shopping. I would not let my moods control me. Sometimes it was quite deliberate, but it worked. Occasionally, my

100

mother would tell me that I wasn't taking care of my daughter, but it didn't upset me. I realized that my mother and I are very different. She is more old fashioned and conventional. I knew being alone for a little while was best for me and for my mental health and I had to stick to that. In turn, being mentally healthy was the best thing for my whole family.

In October, my husband, daughter and mother came to New York. Then my son was born on November 11, 2008. We named him Zohran, which means "emerging star." Although I was a bit emotional for two or three weeks, I didn't have post partum depression or the disconnected feeling I had when my daughter was born. In fact, I bonded with my son instantly. During my pregnancy, because I was alone a lot, I would talk to my son so when he was born I felt very connected to him. That and the fact that I was already a mother made his birth a totally different situation. I finally had the "new mom euphoria."

I also didn't try to take care of him myself – especially with another child to look after. Dr. Birndorf helped me find a baby nurse to care for Zohran when we were still in New York. The whole time I was quite content, feeling like my mental health was getting better every day.

Four months after Zohran was born, I started working out regularly. This was a big deal for me. I've never followed any routine or plan in my entire life. I'd sign up for the gym, but only go once. Or I'd buy a card for ten or fifteen exercise classes and take just one. Even when I hired a trainer at one point, the first thing I told her was, "This isn't going to last long. You should see my track record." But by now, something motivated me and I started exercising like crazy. Even if my trainer didn't come I worked out anyway. I also started eating really healthy food. I was feeling so good about myself, the best I'd felt in years.

What I didn't know was that when I was in New York before my son was born, Abeed and a woman I'll call "L" started their affair. (I'll call her "L" because I don't want her to get any credit in my book. She doesn't deserve that.)

I didn't find out about this affair until two years after it ended. Three of my girl friends told me. One lived in Maryland, one in London and the third in Australia, but they were all in Dhaka at the same time. From the moment they heard about the affair, my friends thought I should know. But they also knew about my illness. Having been around me during the worst of times – my first episode in 1998 - they were truly terrified that news of an affair would trigger a manic episode or nervous breakdown. They cared about me too much for that.

When they finally told me it was my birthday. I know that may sound harsh and horrible, but it was the best birthday gift ever.

"I heard someone say that Abeed is having an affair with L," Radeera said.

So I called the friend she'd heard this from. "Tell me the truth," I said. "Did Abeed have an affair?"

"Can I come to your house?" she said.

"Yes. Let me take a shower first." I know that seems like a weird reaction, but from that moment I knew that it was going to be a long day and I wouldn't have the strength to take a shower later. Once I was dressed and ready, I called my friends and told them to come over. The four of us sat in my living room and they told me everything they knew. I just couldn't believe what I was hearing. It sounds cliché, but I never thought something like this would happen to me. It was like they were telling me someone *else's* story. Not mine. What made it more shocking and excruciatingly painful was that the girl who Abeed cheated with was one of my best friends! She, too, was a married mother and one with three children.

When my friends finished talking, I called Abeed in his office. He was throwing me a big birthday party that night.

"Cancel the party," I said when he picked up the phone.

"What?" he was shocked. After all we had 80 people coming to our house for a party that was all arranged with caterers, music and other festivities.

"Cancel the party and come home right now," I said. When he walked in, I confronted him immediately. Abeed admitted the affair without a split second of hesitation. He didn't even try to hide it. Actually, it seemed like he was relieved that I finally knew. He answered every question I had, giving me any and all the details that I wanted to know.

"Please give me one more chance," he begged in tears. "I'm sorry."

I made Abeed leave the house immediately. After all, I didn't do anything wrong so why should *I* leave? I was angry, shocked, and devastated. My suffering was immense. To say that Abeed had let me down is an understatement. The only way I managed to put on a smiling face through this crisis was because of my two children. I never let them see the pain that I was going through. Why should *they* suffer? This wasn't their fault.

At the time my daughter was six-years-old and my son was two and they didn't know that anything was wrong. Coincidentally, one of my husband's uncles died at the same time so he went away to the funeral. When he returned, I think Abeed had expected my heart to soften, but I was still hurt and betrayed. He was extremely apologetic and it was clear he, too, was suffering for his mistake. Still, I made him sleep upstairs.

Now when I look back, I realized that L was manipulating and using me to get to Abeed. Even before I knew about Abeed's affair, there was something about our friendship that wasn't right. L knew about my bipolar disorder because we'd been friends at the time and at one point during her affair with Abeed she sent me very, very mean texts about my illness. Other times, she would ask me to go out or come over to our house unexpectedly. I remember one night when she called and invited herself over to watch a movie.

"Abeed can drop me later right?" she said.

"Ok," I said, irritated but not thinking much of it.
Another time on our anniversary, L invited herself over to our house and somehow convinced us that she should stay the night. Can you imagine?

Other times, she would try to get me to talk to her about Abeed. "I'm sure the two of you have problems just like every other couple. You must," she'd say. "But you just don't tell me. Right?"

"I don't talk about these things with anyone," I'd say. I remember Abeed telling me that I should stay away from her. I had a fleeting thought that his comment was rather weird, but I let it go.

What's crazy or strange – or both - is that the whole time that L was having this affair with my husband, she was telling me about a love affair she was having with someone in her office. She even gave this fictional lover the same name as my husband! What kind of person would do something like that?

Of course, there were signs early on that she was this type of person, but when you are friends, you tend to overlook a lot. That's what I had done. Then at one point - even before I knew about the affair, I decided that a friendship with L was not one that I wanted to keep. So I started avoiding her. As a result, she began acting very strange. When I didn't come see her children or give her time, she would show up at my house unannounced and cry to me about how important my friendship was to her.

When we came back to New York after my son was born, Abeed started seeing a psychiatrist. He said he was going to deal with all the stress that he was under. I'd had therapists for so many years and saw how much it helped so I didn't question him. In fact, I thought it would help. Later, his therapist became our marriage counselor. At our first session as a couple, I asked the therapist, "Why did Abeed come to see you?"

"Because he was in this messy relationship and he wanted to get out of it," the therapist replied. I later learned that Abeed had tried to end the affair several times. But, devastated at the idea, L was making his life miserable. She went to his office and asked him for money. When he said, "No," she made a huge scene.

"If you don't give me money I'm going to tell this to Nadera," she threatened him. She also tried to use my illness to manipulate Abeed. When he said he was going to tell me about their affair, L would scare him by saying, "But Nadera has a mental illness. If she finds out, she might have a nervous breakdown."

A week after I discovered the affair, I left the country with my children and went to Thailand for ten days. Going away helped me avoid Abeed, my friends and anyone else who knew about this situation. I brought a nanny and asked one of my best friends, Radeera, to come, too. Even though her family was visiting from the United States, she didn't hesitate.

"Of course," she said when I asked her. Although, Radeera knew about the affair, she didn't ask any questions. She knew I didn't want to talk about it. Instead, she gave me exactly what I needed by entertaining my children with trips to the beach and the zoo.

I later came to understand why my friends didn't tell me about Abeed's affair sooner and realized that they did it for my sake. They were genuinely concerned about my mental health. But at the time when they finally *did* tell me, I was very angry with them. *How could they keep this from me?* I wondered. I needed a break from this group of people and anyone remotely involved so I cut myself off completely for several years. When they tried to contact me, I didn't answer their calls. I refused to see or speak to them. They were crazy with worry, wondering what was going on in my life, deeply concerned about my mental state.

To tell you the truth, I don't know how I handled that situation without having a breakdown! But forget about a breakdown, I was cool as a cucumber. Every step that I took, I took calmly. I became like a robot. I did everything perfectly. I was very strong. And, unlike my friends who were seriously concerned, there was not one second when I felt that my mental health was threatened. Everyone around me was shocked – and perhaps worried that I would lose my mind at any minute. However, when I found out about the affair, I was in a very good place. My mental state was strong.

Strangely enough, the timing was actually good because if I had learned of Abeed's affair earlier –even just a year or two, I wouldn't have handled it as well. In the two years since it had happened. I felt so much better about myself and was at peace with my inner self. In fact, I think the strength I gained handling the affair was one of the final steps to healing from my illness. It was just another thing that gave me confidence.

It may sound strange that I turned away from friends who cared about me at a time in my life when I was so devastated and upset. But the truth is, I didn't want to talk about Abeed's affair with anyone. Not my other friends. Not my mother. No one. I even turned away from Dr. Birndorf, who had become my biggest confidant. We had appointments scheduled but I cancelled them. In fact, I didn't talk to her for about two or three months after finding out about the affair.

"I'm not okay, but I don't feel like talking about it right now," I said in my emails. Of course, she was very worried about me. But for me it takes time and I have to be ready to open up. And I wasn't.

I had a huge decision to make about my marriage, my family and my life. It would affect not only me, but my children. And when I have a big decision to make or I'm in a crucial situation, I have to think very independently. Too many interactions with other people distract and confuse me. I like to think alone so I know that whatever decision I make, I made it all by myself without anyone's influence. I wanted to resolve this on my own, with discretion. I didn't want people to say, "You should leave him" or "You shouldn't leave him" or to "do this" or "do that." I can't function if people try and tell me what to do. I felt confident in my ability to make a decision.

Of course it was a difficult time. I was in hell. I was scared. But I was also logical and practical. Thinking of my children gave me the strength to face this crisis. *This is just another problem in my life*, I told myself. *It's a temporary situation and I'll be fine. Time will pass. I'll get through it.* For me, it is the more difficult situations and bigger challenges that are easiest to handle. The small things in life can get me stressed, like what to wear to a dinner or what I should order from the menu. But give me a big problem, a *huge* crisis, and I can handle it.

I'd always had a preconceived idea about cheating. I always thought if my husband had an affair, the answer would be easy. It would be the end of our marriage. I'd get a divorce immediately. Of course, I thought these things because hadn't experienced an affair. It's easy to *think* you'll do something when a situation is hypothetical. It's much different when that situation actually happens to you. Yes, my first reaction was divorce. *I can't live with this person,* I thought. *I'm leaving.* But then I took a step back.

When I got back from Thailand, it had been ten days since I'd spoken to Abeed. The first thing I told him was that we needed to see a marriage counselor. "We can't do this alone," I said. He agreed and arranged everything.

Another thing that got me through this difficult time was taking care of myself. I made sure I slept well –which is very important for managing my illness, exercised and looked good. I didn't sit around in sweatpants, depressed and now showering for days. No. I showered I kept working out, I ate healthy foods and I looked good.

As for L, I never spoke to her again. Friends thought I should call her when I found out about the affair. "Why don't you tell her off?" They asked. "Why don't you ask her how she could do such a thing?" But she wasn't worth it. I didn't want to give her any kind of satisfaction or importance in my life, not one second of my attention. I needed to focus everything on my husband and my family.

A year or so later L's husband died. I don't know if she ever told him about the affair or not. But shortly after his death she called a mutual friend of ours.

"Tell Nadera I'm sorry," she said. "Please tell her to forgive me." I ignored her request. Then recently, L's brother-in-law (her husband's brother) emailed me. "I really want to speak to you. I want to know what actually happened," he wrote. When I didn't reply, he waited a few months and emailed again with the same request.

"Why don't you ask your sister-in-law?" I replied. "Stop bothering me." I heard from friends that he blames L for his brother's death.

I also didn't call my parents when I found out about Abeed's affair. I didn't say anything to them. They were in the States for a few months and I didn't want them to be so far from and so worried. In fact, my mother didn't find out until nine months after I did. Our social circle isn't very big and many people knew about it, so a friend told my mother when she returned to Dhaka.

"I heard this thing about Abeed having an affair. Is it true?" she asked me. She had a concerned look on her face.

"Yes," I replied. "But it happened a long time ago so you don't have to worry about it." I could tell she was very upset so I tried to console her with a saying she used to tell *me*: "G-d puts you into trouble and G-d will get you out of this trouble."

"I'm fine," I added. "There's nothing that I can't handle."

Then she told me a story about our closest family friends. She told me that the husband had an affair with a friend's wife very early in his marriage.

"This kind of thing happens in life," she said. I knew instantly why she was telling me this. The man she was talking about was my favorite family friend. He and his wife had two daughters and one son, whom I was very close to when I was a child. Growing up, I always admired what a tight-knit family they were. They seemed to share a unique closeness that my own family lacked, one that I longed for every time I went to their house. To me, they were the perfect family. So I was shocked and surprised to learn that this man who was like an uncle to me had had an affair and they got through it. I never, ever imagined that anything so troubling had actually happened in their family. I realized that anyone can make mistakes. I also realized that you *can* get through those mistakes and become stronger.

With a lot of effort on both our parts, I realized that could happen for Abeed and I, too. In the end, after a lot of counseling and hard work, I did take him back. Why? Because I saw the bigger picture. Abeed is the father of my children. That is huge. But just as huge is that he had been there for me through many ups and downs. I know I'm not easy to live with and yet, he's stood by me throughout my illness. He had always been protective of me and I don't think I would have come this far if it were not for him standing by me.

And you know what? I actually understand why my husband had an affair. That may sound strange, and I'm not justifying his betrayal, but I do understand to some extent. It's very tough. Temptation is everywhere. There were a couple of times when I could have slipped and done the same thing. At two different points, there were two guys interested in me.

I also take responsibility for my part in his affair, for not giving him the attention he needed. I came from a family where we were used to success in business. It wasn't a big deal. But my husband did not. So when he was doing very well in his business, he wanted to be praised for that and yet I did not appreciate him the way I should. I didn't praise him. It seemed like I was taking him for granted. I'm not saying this is a reason to have an affair, but it was definitely a weakness that was easy for another person to exploit. Admittedly, there was a long period of time during which I had ignored Abeed because I was too focused on my own illness and my recovery. Tthere's no doubt in my mind that this allowed distance to creep in between us. I see now that he felt left out, I was so focused on fixing myself and doing everything properly that I ignored him.

In the end, I did forgive my husband. But it is hard to forget something like that. I don't think I ever will. It has taken great courage to rebuild my trust in our relationship and in my husband. I don't spy on him or check his phone or his email. If it's going to happen again, it's going to happen. There's no point in worrying. I have to trust him - for my children's sake. Neither of us wanted our children to suffer due to this and we both have worked together with that goal in mind.

Everything has a positive side – even Abeed's affair. Yes, even his affair! I used to feel pressure to do everything for his family and impress them. But not anymore. And they don't care. After Abeed's affair, they're just happy I'm here. They realized that it could have been the end of our marriage. After I found out about the affair, I told my father-in-law what happened.

"Whatever you want to do about my son is up to you," he said. Then he told Abeed that whatever I decided about our relationship, he supported. This kind of support and caring strengthened my relationship with my in-laws even more.

In this process I also discovered how many people really care about me. People who before the affair I wouldn't have said are my closest friends. They did so much for me, things I didn't ask for. They were so good to me. I had no idea that so many people cared about me that much and I did not have any expectations from those people. It made me see how truly blessed I am.

It's strange but somehow I feel lighter. I also think his affair improved our marriage. Again, that may sound crazy to some people. But we are much closer now. It hasn't been easy. But neither of us wanted to let go of each other. We made a new resolve to renew our commitments and our relationship has strengthened since then.

Years earlier, before I was married, I was buying books – something I loved to do despite my reading disorder. I also bought a bookmark with what I later learned was the serenity prayer. *God grant us the serenity to accept the things we cannot change, courage to change the things we can, and wisdom to know the difference.* From the second I read it, I loved this quote. It spoke to me. It is such a real thing and it became part of my life. It was also something that helped me get through this horrible time in my life.

Chapter 17

This Life is Beautiful

I live happily in our beautiful home. Where one room is devoted to my love of reading, a vast library that is my sanctuary. My husband and I have two beautiful children, a boy, and a girl. My children are my heroes, they bring so much love and happiness into our lives. It's been amazing to watch them grow from sparkly-eyed children to fun-loving, clever individuals with their own unique personalities. It hasn't always been easy, we have had our ups and downs, but doesn't everyone? We are simply a normal family.

I will be forever grateful to my children, they think I am their hero, but they are mine. They gave me the strength and motivation over the years that I have needed to stay well, they rescued me from falling into the darkest deepest hole and saved me from my illness.

A seed has to die before it can produce a bountiful harvest. And perhaps I had to experience an emotional death. All of the decay and destruction in my life was to be burned away to discover how beautiful my life really was. At first, living with bipolar disorder felt like death, but as I struggled through the years I came to see my illness differently. It was not a door that locked me in and closed me off from experiencing the world in a normal way.

Rather, it was a window, into the manic interpretation of the world and with the shutters held open and the breeze rolling in. I could acknowledge it, even admire the view and then move on.

I'd thought bipolar disorder put me ten years behind in everything. I couldn't do a lot of things that came easily to people of my age. For a long time, I felt like I was in my own world. And yet, in other ways, this illness pushed me forward, full-throttle into the wisdom beyond my years. Teetering on the brink of what felt like the complete destruction of my soul and somehow tumbling out alive has taught me some invaluable lessons about life, for which I would not trade a single moment of the hell I lived through to learn them. I actually see my illness very positively because it posed important challenges for me and taught me many lessons, now today, I deeply appreciate what I took for granted before my illness. Now I appreciate every ounce of my confidence.

There are so many things just waiting to be noticed and enjoyed. If I miss them, I will miss some of the most beautiful gifts that my life can offer – simple things like having a normal conversation with a friend over a cup of tea or interacting with others without feeling anxious and lost; spending an afternoon with my own company, content and without feeling constantly restless. Reading a book, having a sit by the window, in the warm afternoon sun; having a family and a place to call home.

Having this illness has also taught me that I don't have to prove anything to anybody, a feeling that is indescribably liberating. I know who I am and I don't care what other people think.

I learned that I can't be afraid of sorrow, a natural and unavoidable part of life. Instead, I welcome it, a normal, and human, upset. Life is a journey, with ups and downs, twists and turns, gentle hills and massive pot-holes.

Problems will come, without a doubt, but ultimate wisdom is in how to deal with them instead of running away.

I do not regret the struggles but take pride in how they have positively molded my character. My illness has made me strong, patient, insightful, confident and content. It has made me a better person, a better wife, a better sister, daughter, and mother. I know that I would not be the person I am today without my illness.

I now have the ability to recognize the onslaught of a manic episode. I could – can – identify signs and symptoms as they are happening. And instead of caving into them, I acknowledge and take control of them.

I have not let this disease defeat me. The battles were not easy but I was learning how to fight them and stay healthy. I am convinced, now more so than ever, that bipolar disorder was merely a part of me – it did not define me. Finally, I am comfortable in my own skin.

For some people, it takes being 'reborn' like this to realize how beautiful their life really is. At least, that's what it took for me.

When you have gotten through, and you will get through, you will see that every struggle, every challenge, and every tear shed has only made you stronger. Life is too short to constantly ruminate over what you could have done better.

But living a beautiful life is not merely a destination – it is a choice; you don't get any marks just for turning up. I wouldn't change anything about my past. I am who I am today exactly because of the things that happened to me on this journey until the present. Now I have an inner peace, for which I have been longing for years. I know who I am and I don't care what other people think. I realize what life is all about. It's hanging on when your heart has had enough. It's giving more when you feel like giving up. And when you do hang on, when you do give more, life has so much to give you in return: gift upon beautiful gift, just waiting to be opened by a brighter, happier individual. I am that individual, and you can be too.

Printed in Great Britain
by Amazon

43043388R00067

Contents

Pedigree®

Licensed by:

Hasbro

Published by Pedigree Books Limited
Beech Hill House, Walnut Gardens,
Exeter, Devon EX4 4DH
Email:books@pedigreegroup.co.uk
Published 2008
My Little Pony © 2008 Hasbro.

Cheerilee

Cheerilee loves telling stories and working in her garden. She is curious about everything and just loves to share the things she learns...how a flower grows, how a pinwheel turns, how the legends of Ponyville began. She is a very loyal friend and always puts others first. Cheerilee is quite an excitable pony who always has something new to talk about, and often has her friends just as enthusiastic about her discoveries as she is. Cheerilee's favourite thing to do is use her knowledge to help her pony friends find a bright and 'cheery' solution for any situation!

Pinkie Pie

Pinkie Pie is every pony's best friend! She loves throwing parties for every special occasion, particularly her friends' birthdays. Pinkie Pie especially loves balloons of all shapes and sizes, so you can guess what her parties look like! Although Pinkie Pie is very good at planning parties, all the ponies agree that her greatest skill is friendship. She has a warm and loving nature and is always ready to listen and give advice. Ponies often come to Pinkie when they need a little encouragement, some help solving a problem, or just for a friendly hug. And her favourite colour? Pink of course!

PONIES SAVE CHRISTMAS

It was Christmas in Ponyville and all the little ponies were getting ready to celebrate their favourite holiday of the year. It is tradition in Ponyville that each year, one pony is elected to be the Christmas Party Host. This year, the honour was given to Toola-Roola. She was very excited, but also a little nervous. The party the year before had been one of the biggest and best yet and Pinkie Pie, who had been the host, was very proud of it.

"It gives me great pleasure to introduce this year's Christmas Party Host; Toola-Roola!" cried Pinkie Pie to the crowd of Ponies who had gathered around.

Toola-Roola jumped up excitedly and gasped, "Thank you very much, everyone. I only hope that this year's party will be as good as Pinkie Pie's was last year!"

"We are sure it will be, darling," shouted Rainbow Dash from the crowd.

"I hope so," said Toola-Roola as she got down from the makeshift stage that had been erected in Ponyville Square and went to join her friends.

"So Toola-Roola," said Pinkie Pie, "What do you have planned for the party?"

"Well," Toola-Roola replied, "I have made a little list." Toola-Roola opened her bulging purse and a mass of paper sprung out, hitting Pinkie Pie on the nose!

"Wow!" Pinkie Pie exclaimed, rubbing her nose gently, "You have been busy. I'm impressed!"

"Well, I have to admit something," said Toola-Roola as her cheeks grew red with embarrassment, "I have been planning this party for years, I was just waiting for my turn to be the host."

"Oh, Toola-Roola!" laughed the Ponies, "You are funny!"

Pinkie Pie, who loved to throw parties, was longing to get involved. "Toola-Roola, may I see your list? I bet you've got some fantastic ideas. I'm really looking forward to Christmas this year!"
Toola-Roola shook her head and winked, "Pinkie Pie you are the best hostess in Ponyville, but I have been planning this for years: it's top secret!"
The other ponies gathered around Toola-Roola, clamouring to be included in the preparations, but Toola-Roola stood firm.
"There must be loads to do before the party, how can we help?" added Sweetie-Belle.
Toola-Roola grinned and flicked her purse shut around the list, "Oh Sweetie-Belle, I know you are curious, but I want this party to be a surprise. Promise me you won't come to my house until everything's ready?"
The ponies reluctantly agreed and Toola-Roola set off for her house, Sweetie-Belle staring inquisitively after her.

Toola-Roola made her way back to her house, where the party was to be held. Closing the door behind her she looked around, trying to imagine how the party would look.

"Right," she told herself, "I've got a lot to do so I must be organised. If I follow the list everything will be perfect." Toola-Roola pinned the list to the kitchen door and read the first item: Food.

To Toola-Roola, who was more at home mixing paints than ingredients, this task was the most daunting. She took a deep breath and lifted the lid on the Christmas cooking supply box that she had been collecting ever since she had first wanted to host the famous party. Bags of potatoes, bushels of brussel sprouts, carrots, gravy stock, slabs of butter, nuts, chocolate and sacks of flour spilled onto the floor and over Toola-Roola's feet. What a mess!

"At least I don't have to unpack it all!" laughed Toola-Roola as she slid on a carrot. "I'd better get started." Humming merrily, Toola-Roola heaved the largest sack of potatoes to the sink and carefully began to wash them.

Meanwhile, Toola-Roola's friends were in Ponyville Square making snowponies. The snow sparkled in the mid-afternoon sunshine and the sky was pale blue and cloudless. Always energetic, Scootaloo rushed towards the Square, dragging two large red sledges up the hill behind her. Before she even reached her friends, Scootaloo shouted, "Who wants to race first?" Her cheeks were red with effort and her eyes shining in excitement.

But in all the merriment, none of the ponies heard her and as she approached the top of the hill the sledges began to slide and off she shot, straight through the Square and whizzing down the hill to the other side, barely missing the tail of Sweetie-Belle's snowpony.

Sweetie-Belle ran to watch her trying to hold onto one sledge while sitting on the other, and cringed when she saw the huge drift of snow waiting in the valley. The ponies stared while Scootaloo yelled, "Yippeee!" as the sledge she was holding slammed into the snowdrift and the sledge she was riding went skidding to a holt only a metre from a tree. Hair glistening with snowflakes, Scootaloo stumbled dizzily towards Sweetie-Belle, "That was brilliant!" she grinned, "Who's next?"

Soon all the ponies were out of breath from giggling and Sweetie-Belle flopped down on a bench next to Cheerilee. "This is so much fun, I wish Toola-Roola was with us. She must be getting lonely working all alone."
Cheerilee frowned, "Toola-Roola made us promise not to disturb her, Sweetie-Belle. She will be upset if you ruin the surprise."
"I suppose." said Sweetie-Belle, although she was still concerned about her friend.
Since they were all cold and wet from the snow, Pinkie Pie suggested they all went back to her house for some hot chocolate. Sweetie-Belle slowly followed the other ponies towards Pinkie Pie's cottage, and could not resist glancing down the road towards Toola-Roola's house.

Despite the afternoon winter sun, a candle flickered in the kitchen window and Toola-Roola was nowhere to be seen. Sweetie-Belle remembered her promise but decided that asking Toola-Roola if she would like to join their friends for hot chocolate could not possibly ruin the surprise. Feeling only a little guilty, Sweetie-Belle slipped away from the group and skipped quickly down the road.

Toola-Roola heard the doorknocker and came out from the kitchen. She opened the door only a fraction and was about to scold Sweetie-Belle, but Sweetie-Belle didn't give her a chance. "Toola-Roola, you are working so hard here all alone, won't you have a break and join us? I promise not to spoil your surprise," Sweetie-Belle had pulled her woolly hat down so low that here eyes were covered. "I can't see anything! But what is that smell?" Toola-Roola laughed and opened the door properly, "Come in, silly, and take that hat off. There is nothing to see yet!"

SPOT THE DIFFERENCE!

THE FIRST PICTURE HAS FIVE DIFFERENCES FROM THE SECOND. CAN YOU FIND THEM ALL?

1.

2.

1
2
3
4
5

Answers - 1. wrapping paper, 2. fairy light, 3.tree snow, 4. head scarf, 5. Scootaloos ear.

WINTER WORD SEARCH

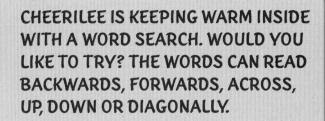

CHEERILEE IS KEEPING WARM INSIDE WITH A WORD SEARCH. WOULD YOU LIKE TO TRY? THE WORDS CAN READ BACKWARDS, FORWARDS, ACROSS, UP, DOWN OR DIAGONALLY.

GOOD LUCK!

- BAUBLE
- SNOW
- HOLLY
- ELVES
- REINDEER
- COLD
- PRESENTS
- FAMILY
- WREATH
- CELEBRATION

G	F	H	H	S	L	K	U	H	N	V	S	W	I	O	A
S	N	O	W	K	L	U	H	B	N	F	R	S	D	G	J
L	Y	L	E	G	V	Y	W	C	K	K	A	A	U	A	J
O	K	L	G	O	P	R	E	S	E	N	N	T	S	L	D
J	D	Y	D	Y	M	E	A	D	I	K	P	B	D	H	E
H	K	F	D	Y	B	N	A	H	K	L	K	H	H	F	T
N	H	J	K	S	H	R	F	G	K	I	J	J	N	B	V
R	E	D	E	G	H	J	H	O	I	B	F	J	G	R	D
E	S	V	V	G	F	R	D	J	E	K	A	N	H	V	B
R	L	E	C	O	L	D	E	I	I	J	H	M	U	H	U
E	N	J	E	E	G	T	F	B	G	T	I	F	R	C	D
I	O	M	L	L	L	I	J	N	B	G	E	L	R	T	D
N	D	E	E	E	D	F	G	T	R	K	Y	L	M	I	T
D	B	G	B	B	D	E	I	Y	K	J	H	G	N	E	R
E	S	D	R	T	F	F	T	C	G	Y	H	D	R	E	F
E	D	K	A	A	F	L	P	O	I	J	E	F	H	N	T
R	V	B	T	H	C	C	R	O	S	A	L	I	E	K	H
G	H	T	I	E	L	G	H	T	D	E	S	E	N	M	B
D	R	T	O	J	G	B	F	D	E	R	F	H	G	I	P
K	K	I	N	Y	H	D	Y	L	I	N	F	S	E	A	B

GUESS THE PONY

★ How well do you know the little ponies?

★ How many can you recognise?

1.

2.

3.

4.

Answers - 1, Rainbow Dash. 2, StarSong. 3, Sweetie Belle. 4, Scootaloo.

COPY AND COLOUR

Scootaloo loves winter because she can go ice-skating. Use the squares as guidelines to help you copy the picture carefully. You can colour Scootaloo the same as the picture or use your favourite colours to design a fab new look!

Rainbow Dash

If you need help picking out the perfect outfit for a special occasion or costume for a play, just ask Rainbow Dash. She is the official glamour girl of Ponyville and can find the perfect look every time! Rainbow Dash is often found at the Fancy Fashions Boutique working on the latest line of sensational dresses, hats, and accessories for the next celebration! Since Ponyville has so much to celebrate, Rainbow Dash is kept busy, but she always has time to help her friends. Rainbow Dash always has good advice on just about everything and also has a very special talent for helping her friends see the more 'colourful' side of the rainbow.

Scootaloo

Scootaloo is always on the go. This fun-loving pony will stop at nothing to make sure everyone is having just as good a time as she is. If she is not organising a game of football or hopscotch, she is gathering a group of pony friends for an exciting day at the amusement park. She loves to get dizzy on the waltzer just before taking a spin on the rollercoaster! Because Scootaloo likes to be involved in every activity throughout Ponyville, she seems to have twice the energy of all her friends and has been known to keep playing even after the other ponies have left! Although she is sporty and active, Scootaloo does occasionally enjoy some quiet time relaxing at the meadow with a collection of fluttering butterflies. As long as she is doing something, Scootaloo is happy.

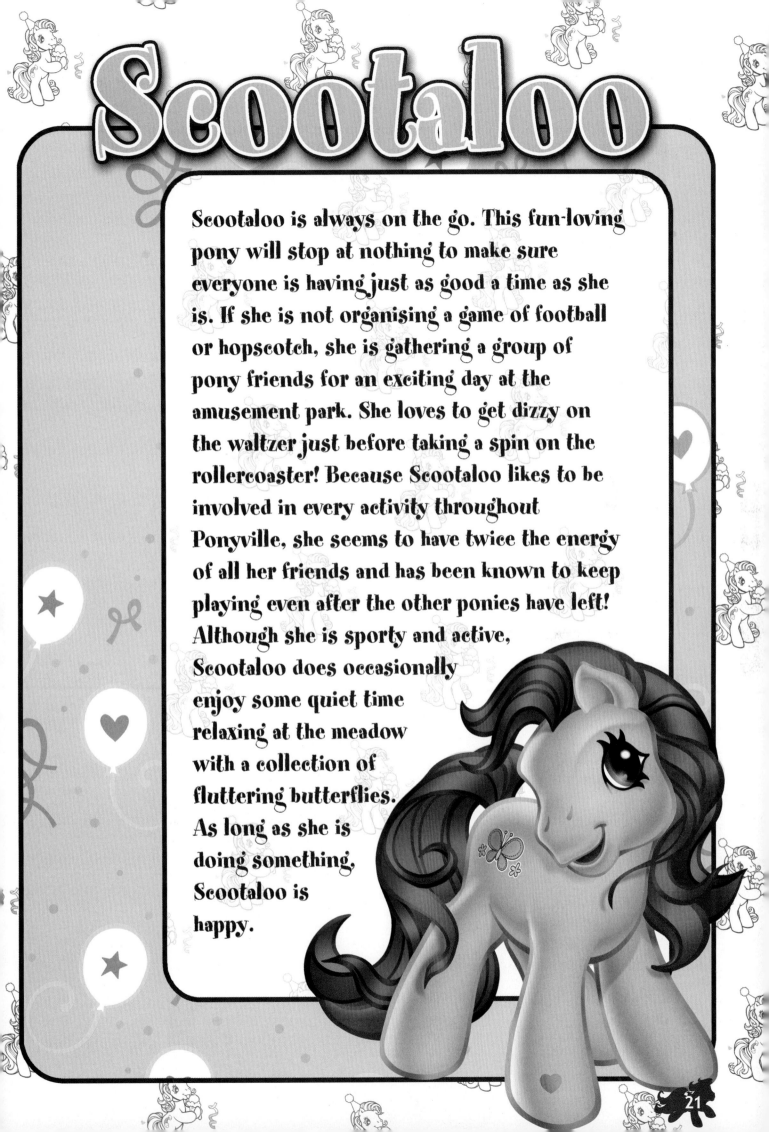

Sweetie-Belle pulled off the hat and shook the hair from her eyes. "You look like a ghost!" She giggled, and when Toola-Roola saw her reflection she laughed too. She had been cooking, but it seemed that more of the ingredients had ended up on her face than in the mixing bowl. Her usually gold and pink hair was white with flour and she had four raisins stuck behind her ear with what Sweetie-Belle thought was maple syrup.

Sweetie-Belle followed Toola-Roola into the kitchen and suddenly Toola-Roola's appearance made sense. The cupboard doors were open, their contents spilling onto the table. Buckets on the floor contained vegetables in various states of peeling, soaking and straining. The sink was buried under potato peel and what little of the table was visible was covered in flour, wet pastry and bowls of icing and sweets. There was a recipe book propped open behind the tap, but its pages were smothered behind another layer of flour and sugar.

Sweetie-Belle stared and Toola-Roola blushed.
"I might have got mixed up." Toola-Roola explained. "I've been planning this meal for years but I didn't realise how difficult cooking everything at once is. How did Pinkie Pie do it?"
Sweetie-Belle picked a carrot from a mound of glacier cherries and returned it to the colander that balanced unsteadily behind them. "Well, last year I helped Pinkie Pie cook, and we certainly didn't do it all at once!"
Sweetie-Belle did not want to upset Toola-Roola, so she asked as nicely as she could, "I would like to stay if you don't mind some company."
Toola-Roola opened her mouth, then glanced around her at the mess and sighed, "Yes please, Sweetie-Belle, I don't think I can do all this cooking alone."
So Sweetie-Belle put on an apron and together the two friends began to start the recipes again.

23

At Pinkie Pie's house the ponies were happily discussing their plans. Christmas Eve was an important occasion in Ponyville as the whole village gathered to sing carols in the Square followed by a procession to light the candles on the Christmas tree. This year the tree would be in Toola-Roola's house and it was, of course, a surprise. None of the ponies had seen Toola-Roola take a tree into the house and Scootaloo quietly asked if maybe she had forgotten.
"I'm sure she hasn't," said StarSong, "You saw the list!"
But all the same, the ponies fell quiet. Toola-Roola did not want anyone to interfere but the Christmas Eve celebration would be ruined without a tree.

StarSong suggested they practise the carols for the evening, and Rainbow Dash agreed, "Toola-Roola is working very hard and we must too. She is preparing this whole party herself so one missing tree would not be a disaster." Gathered around StarSong, who wanted to practise her Silent Night solo, the ponies tried to forget about the tree and concentrate on singing. Scootaloo fidgeted as she looked out the window. She found it hard to stand still and sing quietly while the last hour of daylight faded and she knew she could not play outside after dark.

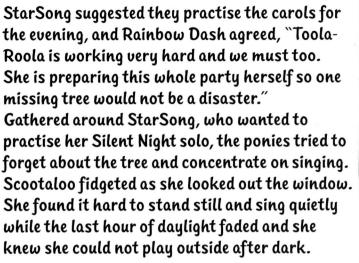

During a brief argument about the volume needed for a certain fa la la, Scootaloo tiptoed out of the house and into the village.

The sun was setting behind the castle and the leafless trees were lined with snow and their branches drooped as if the snow weighed far more than leaves. Scootaloo shivered.
"There's no point getting cold; she will either be pleased to see me or not and I won't find out any faster standing here in the snow." She told herself and hurried to Toola-Roola's house.

26

The candle in the kitchen window was burning low when Scootaloo arrived and inside she could hear footsteps after her nervous knock.

Toola-Roola opened the door and said nothing, looking sternly at Scootaloo.

Scootaloo ignored her scowl and said cheerfully, "Hello Toola-Roola, how are you getting on? I thought you might like some help."

"This party is meant to be a surprise!" Toola-Roola replied, "We are working hard and everything will be ready. Now go away before you see something you shouldn't."

Scootaloo smiled and repeated, "We?"

Toola-Roola's face fell into her usual smile, "Well, Sweetie-Belle is here helping me cook." She admitted. "But we have a lot to do so we can't have any more distractions."

Scootaloo was pleased that Toola-Roola wasn't alone after all and smiled back.

"Okay, but don't be late for the Christmas Eve carols. The procession is starting in the Square at seven."

"Thank you, we won't!" said Toola-Roola and was about to close the door when she realised, "Oh no, Scootaloo! I haven't put the tree up! It's in the garden and it's far too big to carry between just two ponies. How did Pinkie Pie manage last year?"

Scootaloo's eyes widened; just how big was this tree? "Don't worry," she said confidently, "I got the tree last year. I will help."

27

The tree was huge. Its trunk was in a pretty red pot which was tastefully wrapped with gold ribbon. But the tree itself was so tall that it lay half on the ground and half on the sledge Toola-Roola had used to transport it from the forest.

"Wow!" exclaimed Scootaloo, "That's a beautiful tree. It's going to look fabulous with all the decorations and candles on."

Sweetie-Belle had joined them, "It's enormous." She agreed.

Toola-Roola stood at the base of the tree and the others positioned themselves further down so she could lead them to the correct place inside. "One, two, three...lift!"

Groaning slightly as if it too was trying to help lift, the tree came up and the three friends shuffled it indoors.

"Phewf," said Sweetie-Belle as they balanced the tree upright in the corner of the party room. "Those pine needles smell lovely but they do stick into your hair!"
Scootaloo laughed and shook her head, showering Sweetie-Belle with more pine needles.
The three stood back to catch their breath and admire the tree.
Toola-Roola opened her mouth and closed it again, grinning to herself and wriggling on the spot. "What's wrong? Pine needles?" Sweetie-Belle asked her.
Toola-Roola smiled, "No, I have a lovely surprise for the tree and I don't want to spoil it, but I am so excited I suppose telling just you two won't do any harm."
Sweetie-Belle and Scootaloo looked happily at each other; they knew Toola-Roola couldn't keep a secret when she was that excited and they were pleased to be the first to know.

Ponies' Palette

Look how much fun Toola-Roola and Rainbow Dash are having making snowponies! Each number shows which colour that area should be. Follow the numbers to complete the picture.

1) Green
2) Red
3) Yellow
4) Pink
5) MediumPink
6) Dark Pink
7) Light Blue
8) MediumBlue
9) Dark Blue
10) Light green
11) orange
12) Brown
13) White/Blue

Christmas Maze

Ponyville looks so different covered in snow and ice! Help Pinkie Pie find her friends.

Sweetie-Belle's Mini Christmas Puddings

Sweetie-Belle loves cooking and decorating delicious treats for her friends. Ask an adult to help you make her mini Christmas puddings.

Pudding Ingredients:

185g/3oz unsalted butter
110g/4oz plain chocolate
85g/3oz raisins (or sultanas)
2 tbsp orange juice
370g/13oz ready-made ginger cake

Method:

1. Soak the raisins (or sultanas) in orange juice for about half an hour.
2. Melt the butter and chocolate either over a pan of simmering water or in a microwave.
3. Stir in the raisins (or sultanas) and the liquid, then crumble in the cake.
4. Mix and leave to cool slightly. Place in the fridge for about 1 hour to firm up, then roll into 10 walnut-sized balls.

Decoration:

30g/1oz ready-to-roll icing
green and red food colouring
tube of red writing icing

Method:

1. Colour 1/3 of the icing green, roll out on a surface dusted with icing sugar and cut into holly leaves.
2. Colour 1/3 of the icing red and roll into berries.
3. Roll out the remaining white icing and cut into circles for the top of the cakes.
4 Dampen the underneath of the icing to stick it to the cake. Place the white on first for snow, then add the holly.

THIS ACTIVITY REQUIRES ADULT SUPERVISION

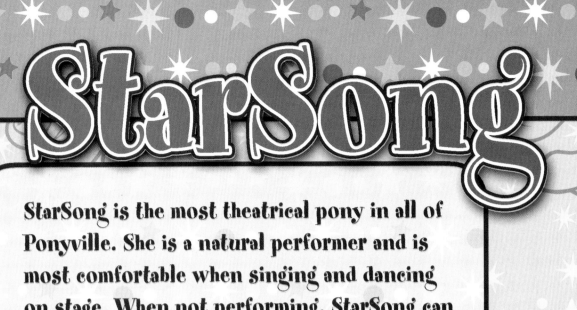

StarSong

StarSong is the most theatrical pony in all of Ponyville. She is a natural performer and is most comfortable when singing and dancing on stage. When not performing, StarSong can be found managing the Ponyville theatre, teaching dance lessons and preparing for the next big production. StarSong puts her heart into everything she does and will spend hours practising until she reaches her own high standards. She loves spending time with her pony friends but often gets caught up in her busy production schedule. Not to worry, StarSong's friends often bring the fun to the theatre and offer a helping hand with costumes, set design and joining in the show!

Sweetie-Belle

Sweetie-Belle is a very sweet and thoughtful young unicorn. Even though she is a bit clumsy at times and her curiosity sometimes gets her into trouble, Sweetie-Belle always has the best intentions with everything she does. She loves to bake cupcakes and all sorts of sweet treats for everyone to enjoy. Sweetie-Belle's friends are extremely important to her and she can't stand anyone being miserable. Sweetie-Belle's kindness can always bring a smile to any pony's face, as can her cakes! She can usually be found in the Ponyville Sweet Shop where her friends often drop in to visit her and try a sample. In fact, it smells so delicious it is hard to walk past without going in!

Toola-Roola led them to the attic stairs saying, "I've been working on this since the summer," before she vanished up into the attic. Reappearing a minute later slightly dustier than before, Toola-Roola was carrying a large brown box with a red ribbon.

In the party room Toola-Roola opened the box and carefully lifted out a gorgeous golden star which had tiny star shaped holes through which the glow of a small candle would shine.

"Beautiful" Toola-Roola's friends agreed.

"I have some candles, baubles and tinsel for the rest of the tree, but I thought this could go right on top." Toola-Roola explained.

Scootaloo looked at the delicate star and then up at the top of the tree, towering above her. "How?" She asked simply.

The three ponies stared up at the tree which was bending slightly, even under the party room's high ceiling, and Toola-Roola groaned, "I don't know!"

"Where is Sweetie-Belle? She hasn't sung at all!" said StarSong, looking around the rehearsal.
"Neither has Scootaloo," said Cheerilee who found singing quietly a little dull and was annoyed that the two ponies seemed to have escaped StarSong's enthusiasm.
"They must be with Toola-Roola." StarSong said, "Although I don't think Toola-Roola will be very pleased. It is only one hour until the carol procession, I hope they aren't getting in the way."
Rainbow Dash and Pinkie Pie looked at each other; they knew what was coming.
"Maybe I had better check on them," said StarSong.
No one answered; they were all curious about the secretive preparations and perhaps StarSong would come back with news.

StarSong flew quickly to Toola-Roola's house, enjoying the twinkling of the first evening stars in the inky sky. Before she had even reached the door, the sound of a slow crash came from within the house. This was shortly followed by laughter and an "Ouch!"

"Hello?" Called StarSong as she peered inside, "Toola-Roola? Can I come in?" There was no answer except more laughing, so StarSong went to the party room. Toola-Roola and Sweetie-Belle were underneath the enormous Christmas tree which was lying on its side again and only Scootaloo's ears were visible between the branches and the golden star, which seemed wedged on her head.

"What are you doing?" StarSong giggled as she helped Toola-Roola up.

"Oh no, StarSong! You're not meant to see the star until the party! Close your eyes!" Toola-Roola exclaimed and leapt over to Scootaloo, whose face was still stuck in the ornament.
 Sweetie-Belle climbed out of the tree and looked at the mess. "Shall we try to put it back up?" She asked sceptically.
There was a faint popping sound as Scootaloo's left ear popped out, freeing the star. "Definitely. I want to try that again."
"Scootaloo, no, climbing the tree didn't work." Toola-Roola gently took the star from Scootaloo who was jiggling around trying to get rid of more pine needles.
Just then a bell sounded in the kitchen.
"The cakes!" exclaimed Sweetie-Belle, "And the biscuits! And I must turn the puddings!" She vanished into the kitchen.
Toola-Roola looked sadly at the star. "I suppose we could put it on the table instead. It'll look just as pretty there." She said, even though she didn't really think it would. "I wish I knew how Pinkie Pie got her star so high up last year."
"Nonsense." replied StarSong, "Last year I put the star up with Pinkie Pie. If we work together now we can manage." She took the star from Toola-Roola's hands and wedged it firmly on the top of the tree. "Now let's try to lift it. One, two, three..."

Slowly, and with much panting, they angled the tree upright. The star was almost touching the ceiling but it stayed on. Toola-Roola, Scootaloo and StarSong had to crane their necks to see, but the star looked beautiful.

Sweetie-Belle returned from the kitchen and gasped, "Well done!"

Toola-Roola smiled then looked at the list on the kitchen door. There was less than an hour to go until all of Ponyville arrived and she began to worry again.

"There isn't much time, StarSong, and I do want everything to be perfect," Toola-Roola said.

"I don't know how Pinkie Pie did it!"

StarSong smiled, "Last year I helped Pinkie Pie with the decorations. I would love to help you too, if I'm not in the way."

When StarSong didn't return to Pinkie Pie's house the other ponies became worried. Sweetie-Belle, Scootaloo and now StarSong had all vanished to Toola-Roola's house even though they had promised not to go. Pinkie Pie wondered if anything was wrong.

"Darling, I'm sure its fine," Rainbow Dash said. "But perhaps we had better check."

Cheerilee nodded, "We promised not to, but it won't do any harm to just pass by and make sure Toola-Roola is okay."

"We shouldn't all go; we don't want Toola-Roola to think we think she can't manage, and she really did want to prepare the party alone." Pinkie Pie said. "Rainbow Dash, you go, it was your idea. Cheerilee and I will gather the candles for the carol procession."

Rainbow Dash nodded and was already up and out of the door before Cheerilee and Pinkie Pie could even say `Goodbye'.

When Rainbow Dash arrived at Toola-Roola's house, there were candles in every window and she could see four ponies hurrying around, so blurred by speed she couldn't tell who was who. She knocked on the door and waited, staring firmly at her feet to avoid peeking through the windows and ruining the surprise.

Toola-Roola opened the door and did not even seem surprised. "Come in, Rainbow Dash, you might as well look; everyone else has." She said quietly.

Rainbow Dash stepped slowly into the house and breathed deeply. Scents of cinnamon, sugar, and warm bread drifted from the kitchen. The dusky smells of holly, pine and mistletoe mingled from the party room where StarSong was hanging huge garlands and wreaths as she kicked empty boxes and unused ribbons out of the way. The star glistened and its candle reflected a hundred times in each brightly coloured bauble that Scootaloo hung on the tree.

Sweetie-Belle passed them carrying a large bowl with a red and white striped tea towel draped over it. She slipped on the holly berries that StarSong had dropped and skidded to the table before dropping the bowl heavily onto a green and gold tablecloth. The tea towel did not quite contain the smell and Rainbow Dash longingly imagined which of Sweetie-Belle's delicious specialities could be in the bowl. Toola-Roola was draped in armfuls of tinsel and paper chains, which she was wrapping round doors, chair legs, picture frames, the grandfather clock and anything else she could reach. There was hardly a centimetre of the room which didn't contain something Christmassy.

Toola-Roola

Toola-Roola is Ponyville's favourite artist. She loves to do arts and crafts of all kinds, the messier the better! She always has a dab of paint on her nose or a bit of glitter in her hair! Toola-Roola's friends are always welcome to stop by her art studio to draw, paint, sculpt or just watch as she creates a new and exciting work of art. Toola-Roola is always there to offer creative inspiration or to help guide the talents of an aspiring pony artist. Toola-Roola is ambitious and always wants everything she creates to be the best it can. She also loves helping her friends fulfil their creative potential. In fact, her greatest joy is time spent using her skills to help the other ponies with their special talents, like helping Star Song create fabulous sets or decorating the most beautiful cakes with Sweetie-Belle!

Odd One Out

Something is missing from one of these pictures, can you find where? Use your favourite colours to complete the pictures. Whether you colour them all the same or differently is up to you!

1.

2.

3.

4.

Answer - '3' is the odd one out.

Make your own Christmas Decorations!

Making your own Christmas decorations is a fantastic way to make your celebration special, it's also great fun!

Toola-Roola's Paper Chain

You will need:

Coloured paper (or an old magazine) cut into rectangles and glue.

Choose your coloured paper and ask an adult to help you cut it into rectangles.

Tip: to make them easy to glue together, the rectangles should be twice as long as they are wide.

Glue the ends of one rectangle together to make a hoop.

Put the next rectangle through the hoop then glue the ends together.

Repeat these steps until your chain is long enough!

Toola-Roola's Paper Angels

You will need:

Paper
Scissors

Tip: long angel chains can be difficult to colour in. Why not try using coloured paper?

Fold the paper like an accordion so that all sections are equal.

On the top section draw an angel whose hands reach the edges.

Ask an adult to help you cut carefully around the angel, except the hands.

Open out your paper and you will have a row of angels holding hands!

Dot-to-Dot

What is Scootaloo doing?

Join the dots to find out.

Then you can colour in the picture.

Put Scootaloo's cutie marks on the pony!

Hide and Seek

Pinkie Pie is planning to surprise her friend StarSong by hiding pretty balloons.

How many can you find?

"Darling, this is wonderful!" Rainbow Dash cried and gave Toola-Roola a big hug, tinsel and all. Toola-Roola squirmed and said awkwardly, "But there is still tidying much to do, and it is almost time for the Christmas Eve carol procession. I should have known I couldn't prepare the most important celebration in Ponyville."

Although she was speaking quietly, everyone stopped still and looked at her. She stood covered in tinsel and paper chains amidst strewn boxes and dropped pine needles.

"There just isn't time." Toola-Roola finished and started to cry.

The four ponies rushed to comfort their friend and look around the room. They could see what she meant; it was a mess. But under the mess they could see that the room looked beautiful.

"Toola-Roola, don't cry," said Rainbow Dash. "Now everything is ready we only have to tidy up, and with five of us here that won't take long."

"I thought I could do it alone," Sniffed Toola-Roola, "But I couldn't. I hope Pinkie Pie isn't too disappointed in me. I don't know how she made such a lovely party last year."

Rainbow Dash looked at the tinsel and paper chains that still hung round Toola-Roola's neck and had an idea. Thoughtfully, she looked around the room again. "I know why Pinkie Pie's party was such a success." She said and handed Toola-Roola a tissue. "Pinkie Pie had help with the cooking from Sweetie-Belle, Scootaloo brought a tree from the forest, StarSong decorated with the garlands and wreaths she made and we were all at Pinkie Pie's house for hours adding the finishing touches." Looking at Toola-Roola's tinsel and paper chains, she added, "I remember you hanging those decorations last year, too."

Toola-Roola looked down in surprise and held up a bright red paper chain as if seeing it for the first time. "You're right." She said slowly. "I did help Pinkie Pie last year, and so did everybody else. I had been planning this party for so long that I had forgotten how much hard work it is. I thought I could impress Ponyville by preparing everything myself, but the best thing about the Ponyville Christmas Party is seeing everyone's hard work come together." Toola-Roola looked ashamed and reached to hug her friends. "I'm sorry I said I didn't want your help."

"Darling!" Said Rainbow Dash and they all hugged Toola-Roola.

"There's still time!" Shouted Scootaloo and suddenly the house was in mayhem. The five ponies raced around gathering empty boxes, tidying away pots and pans, laying out plates for Sweetie-Belle's treats and adding the last few decorations to the tree. Just as Toola-Roola shut the last box into the attic and Sweetie-Belle wiped the last stray smudge of flour from her cheek, the grandfather clock chimed. It was time for the Christmas Eve procession and, against all Toola-Roola's predictions, the party was ready. Laughing excitedly, the ponies took another satisfied look at the beautiful room and ran happily back up to the Square.

All the ponies of Ponyville were waiting in the Square amongst the snowponies they had made earlier. In the dusk the snowponies looked almost real, although it was easy to tell them apart from the ponies, because they were all so excited that they couldn't keep still. Each pony was holding a candle and as Toola-Roola, Sweetie-Belle, Scootaloo, StarSong and Rainbow Dash approached Cheerilee greeted them with a smile and handed them each a candle to carry. Pinkie Pie was standing on the stage which had been there since the announcement and beckoned Toola-Roola to join her as everyone took their places in the procession.

"Ponies, as you know, this year Toola-Roola has prepared the Christmas Party. Let's give her a round of applause!"

All the ponies clapped as, blushing, Toola-Roola climbed onto the stage.

Looking around at all her friends, Toola-Roola thought how lucky she was. Even though she had been stubborn, her friends only wanted the best for her and the party. The best way to celebrate Christmas is with the people you love and Toola-Roola was grateful she hadn't spent the day alone.

Taking a deep breath she said, "I wanted to prepare the best Christmas party Ponyville had ever seen, and I wanted to impress you by doing it alone. This Christmas I have learnt that friends want to help each other and I am very grateful. Merry Christmas everyone!"

"Merry Christmas!" They all replied.

Over the silence of the snowy night, the sound of the Ponyville Christmas carols began. StarSong led the candlelit procession through the village to Toola-Roola's house. The ponies gasped in delight at the sight of the party room and their happy faces added the most important decoration. The enormous Christmas tree stood proudly in the corner, Toola-Roola's golden star glowing regally on top. To the delicate sound of StarSong's Silent Night, the ponies carefully placed their candles on the Christmas tree and eagerly awaited the special day with their friends. Looking around the beautiful party room, the ponies congratulated Toola-Roola. She had wanted to prepare the best Christmas party Ponyville had ever seen and, with the help of her friends, she had.

Thank You Letter

Toola-Roola is grateful to her friends for helping her this Christmas. Use this template to say 'thank you' to your loved ones.

Dear

My favourite part of Christmas was

Thank you for

Love from

Friends Forever!

Show your friends how much they mean to you with this personalised jewellery. You could even make them together.

You will need:
four coloured embroidery threads or wool 70cm long.

Tie the threads together with a knot 6cm from the ends (you will use this to tie the bracelet to your friend's wrist).

Stick the short ends to a table with sellotape or ask your friend to hold them tight.

Loop thread A (far left) over and under thread B. Hold thread B straight and pull the knot tight. Repeat this to make a double knot.

Keep doing this until the pattern is long enough to go around your friend's wrist.

Take thread B and tie double knots around each of the other threads going from left to right.

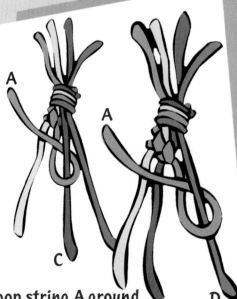

Loop string A around threads C and D in the same way. Now thread A is on the far right.

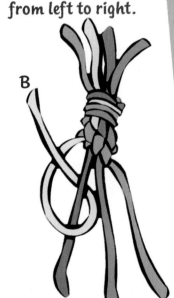

Tie the remaining threads together with a knot, leaving about 6cm at the end.

59

RACE TO THE CASTLE

StarSong was having so much fun at the theatre that she didn't notice it was getting dark! Race with her to the castle.

You will need: counters and a dice.

If you land on StarSongs's special star spots you can move forward 2 extra spaces, but if you land on a dangerous dark spot miss a turn while you find your way.

Begin

1 2 3

4

5

12 11 10

13 9 7 6

15 16 17 18 19 20

39 40 41

38 42

End

35 36

33

32 31 30 29 28

27

21 23 24 25 26